Robert Louis Stevenson

A Critical Celebration

Robert Louis Stevenson

A Critical Celebration

Edited by

Jenni Calder

Barnes & Noble Books
Totowa, New Jersey

First published in the USA 1980 by

Barnes & Noble Books
81 Adams Drive
Totowa, New Jersey, 07512

ISBN 0—389—20145—6

Printed in Scotland

Contents

A Spirit Intense and Rare

JENNI CALDER

When W.E. Henley wrote his well-known sonnet on Robert Louis Stevenson he caught arrestingly something of the mixture of conflicting elements that made up his personality.

> *The brown eyes radiant with vivacity —*
> *There shines a brilliant and romantic grace,*
> *A spirit intense and rare, with trace on trace*
> *Of passion and impudence and energy.*

And also, Henley went on to say, he was 'sternly critical', with much of the Antony and the Hamlet in his character, and 'something of the Shorter-Catechist'. The continuing fascination of Stevenson lies not only in his attractiveness as a writer, but in the charm and the paradox of his personality.

When Stevenson died in Samoa, at the early age of forty-four, the literary world, the reading public in general, and particularly his close friends and associates, felt his loss like the sudden dimming of a light: 'this ghastly extinction of the beloved R.L.S.', as Henry James put it. He had been hailed in his lifetime not only as a major writer, but as a writer who had revitalised literature. Many felt that after the achievements of the Victorian period's major novelists — Dickens, Thackeray, George Eliot — writing had fallen into a rather tedious recital of everyday details. What was looked for was excitement, fantasy and drama that would transport the reader into an inspiring world of dreams. Stevenson, many felt, was the man to do that.

It was not only just the loss of an inspiring writer that was mourned. It was the loss of a sparkling and sympathetic personality, a man of wit, of kindness, of warmth and humour, who made an impact, usually favourable, on everyone he met. He was one of the most attractive literary figures there have ever been. His friend Edmund Gosse spoke of him as 'the most entrancing personality he had ever come across', and E.F. Benson, who recorded this comment, described how 'he cast over his friends a glamour which they confess entirely dazzled them'.

Many people recorded their impressions of this man, eager to claim acquaintance with the promising but prematurely dead author. Part of the dazzle arose from the brilliance of his conversation. He loved to talk, and as he talked he would move about the room, gesturing expressively, smoking almost continuously, fluid and restless. 'There was positively a sort of radiance about him, as if emanating from his genius', wrote another, P.G. Hamerton, of his meeting with him. He was spontaneous and thoroughly unconventional. In a letter Barrie describes how as a student he encountered Stevenson once, not knowing who he was, in the middle of Princes Street in Edinburgh. Stevenson at once whisked him off to his favourite tavern, Rutherford's, in Drummond Street (it is still there) and substituted several hours of brilliant conversation for the university class Barrie should have been attending. Sometimes his friends were embarrassed by his unpredictable behaviour, but the Stevenson magic almost always worked, and diverted their annoyance.

He has often been described as a man who never grew up, who retained a boyish charm in his personality and his writing that was an essential part of his effect. (He may have contributed something to Barrie's Peter Pan.) But this scarcely does him justice. He was a man of sophisticated moral feeling and a profound sense of responsibility. He cared deeply about the iniquities of the world in which he lived, disliked hypocritical attitudes, and was acutely sensitive to the moral predicaments men and women inevitably found themselves in. The rigid Calvinism of his Edinburgh upbringing had its effect. Although he reacted against its negative character it marked his outlook on human behaviour and flavoured almost everything he wrote. Those who knew him well were very much aware of this.

Stevenson longed for life to be full of colour and drama. In his early twenties he wrote in a letter to his mother, 'I wish that life were an opera. I should like to *live* in one, but I don't know in what quarter of the globe I shall find life so constituted . . . imagine asking for three Kreuzer cigars in recitative, or giving the washerwoman an inventory of your dirty clothes in a sustained and flourishing aria.' He loved the theatre — he participated energetically in amateur theatricals — and he loved music because they could transpose ordinary life onto a different plane, where everything was bigger and brighter and richer in expression. This desire to magnify and intensify the ordinary features of life went back to his boyhood games with Skelt's model theatre and cutout figures and scenes. He would paint them and arrange them on the tiny stage, enacting hair-raising adventures: his youthful version of life as an opera.

Stevenson grew up in Edinburgh, the only child of a solidly professional and strictly Calvinist family. His birth in 1850, exactly half way through the century, has a neatly symbolic significance. He was very much the child of the second half of the nineteenth century, his adult thinking shaped by a reaction against the bourgeois achievements of the mid-Victorian period and by the new ideas that were challenging conventional Christianity. Stevenson, although he has been beloved by the establishment, was very much a part of the rebellion which rippled through the last quarter of the century, against solid Victorian virtues. At the same time, he loved and respected his parents greatly, and was agonised by his disagreements with them.

Thomas Stevenson, his father, was a lighthouse and harbour engineer, successful and much respected in the city of Edinburgh. His mother, born Margaret Isabella Balfour, was the daughter of a Church of Scotland minister. They were devoted to their son, an anxious devotion because he was so often ill. He succumbed not only to all the usual illnesses of childhood, which were at that time rather more numerous and more dangerous than they are now, but at an early age showed a tendency to chest ailments which would eventually, in adulthood, become the terrifying haemorrhaging that seemed to signify turberculosis.

Stevenson was born and brought up in the elegantly laid out crescents and terraces of Edinburgh's New Town, living from the age of six in Heriot Row, one of the finest of the city's Georgian streets. With his devoted nurse Alison Cunningham, whom he called 'Cummy', he walked through the streets largely occupied by members of the professions, played in the iron-railed gardens across the

R.L.S. aged 4

road from his home, explored the Water of Leith which ran through the New Town's northern perimeter, and made fascinated excursions to Warriston cemetery. He never lost his predilection for graveyards.

Often he was not well enough to go out at all. For weeks on end he would be in bed, feverish, sleepless, his vivid imagination conjuring up bright and often terrifying images gleaned from the stories his nurse and his parents had told him, from the Bible, from folk tales and from the adventure stories his father loved to invent. Fever and long

The Stevenson family, R.L.S. second from right

days and nights spent inactive gave his mind vast scope for self-entertainment; later he remembered, 'the unnatural activity of my mind after I was in bed at night'. The rigorous Calvinism by which he was surrounded was also a stimulant. At a very early age he frightened himself by brooding on sin and had frequent nightmares about damnation and the devil. Those early imaginings directly fed his adult stories.

Stvenson's growing up is reflected in his *Child's Garden of Verses*, written in his early thirties. The volume is usually thought of as being full of the innocent delights of childhood, but although childish pleasures are celebrated there are also poems about the less pleasant aspects of youthfulness, about loneliness, about the shadows of the night — 'the haunted night returns again' — about isolation from the world of adults. His own memoirs indicate that he had mixed feelings about his childhood, which is perhaps why he wrote so sympathetically for children. 'I have been happier since,' he wrote of his childhood, 'for I think most people exaggerate the capacity for happiness of a child; but I have never again been happy in the same way.'

Many of his best times were spent just on the fringe of the city at Colinton Manse, the house of his maternal grandfather, Dr Lewis Balfour. The manse, with its large and varied garden, was beside the Water of Leith, and the river, the garden with its trees and shrubs, and the neighbouring graveyard, offered much scope for imaginative games. Stevenson wrote about it later, celebrating the sounds of water and mills, 'the wheel and the dam sighing their alternate strain; the birds on every bush and from every corner of the overhanging woods pealing out their notes until the air throbbed with them . . .' Colinton meant more freedom than was possible at Heriot Row, as did the summer holiday visits to North Berwick on the coast and to the Borders, where the young Louis, as he was always known, although the original spelling was 'Lewis', after his grandfather, could enjoy the companionship of friends and cousins on beach and hillside.

His schooling was frequently interrupted for long periods, and he never distinguished himself as a scholar. Thomas Stevenson had no other thought but that his son should join his own profession, and in 1867 Louis began his studies at the University of Edinburgh with engineering in mind. But it was already clear to Louis, if not to his parents, that his real interests did not take him in that direction. He had been spending much of his time writing. When he accompanied his father on lighthouse inspection tours round the coast of Scotland he responded not to the triumphs of nineteenth century engineering but to the wildness, the gaunt beauty, the challenge of terrain and the elements, that he was experiencing. Crossing wild Magus Moor, the scene of the murder of Archbishop Sharp, a precipitating event in the Covenanting wars of the seventeenth century, Louis, only thirteen at the time, fed his imagination on the sinister and stark event, the cloaked horsemen pursuing the Archbishop's carriage, the murder done in cold blood by men fanatically convinced of the rightness of their cause.

The Covenanters, cruelly fighting a righteous war and prepared to die for their religious freedom, always fascinated him. It was an aspect of the Scottish past that

8 Howard Place, Edinburgh

gripped him all his life, more than the numerous events in Scottish history that could be transformed into more colourfully heroic fiction. The Covenanting wars were a sombre episode. Stevenson would often walk on the Pentland Hills and brood over the scene of the Covenanters' defeat at Rullion Green in 1666. It was a favourite spot of his, and in the last years of his life his thoughts often turned to the grey-green Pentland slopes and Glencorse churchyard with its plain stone monuments to the dead. One of his most moving poems records his deep emotional links with the place and its history:

*Blows the wind today, and the sun and the wind
are flying,
    Blows the wind on the moor today and now,
Where above the graves of the martyrs the
whaups are crying,
        My heart remembers how!*

He wrote that poem towards the end of his life, thousands of miles away from the Pentland Hills in the South Pacific.

By the time Louis went to university his rebellious and bohemian tendencies were apparent. He was much encouraged in those directions by his slightly older cousin R.A.M. Stevenson, who would later become a well-known art critic. Bob was a flamboyant character, usually described as being like Louis only more so. He was full of charm and spontaneity, vigorously unconventional, and high-spirited. For Louis he was an inspiring companion, and although Louis's parents were convinced later that Bob was responsible for leading him seriously astray in fact he was helping Louis to find the courage of his own convictions.

As a student Louis soon acquired a certain notoriety. He walked about the city, long-haired, dressed in black shirt and neckerchief and velvet jacket, standard bohemian garb of the time but not common in Edinburgh, avidly interested in the underside of the city's life. On the surface life in Edinburgh was God-fearing, respectable and well-conducted. But, like every large Victorian city, beneath this was an underworld of very different character, of criminals and prostitutes and drop-outs, who frequented the areas of the city on the fringe of the bourgeois terraces and the expanding villas to the south of the Old Town. Stevenson was vividly aware of the physical as well as of the moral contrasts of the town, and described them memorably in his book *Edinburgh: Picturesque Notes*. The overcrowded and insalubrious Old Town, with its dramatic skyline of castle, cathedral and tall tenements, looked down over the gracious monotony of the New. As a student Stevenson made his way up from Heriot Row to the University, an academic island in the midst of the seething life of the old part of the city. He frequented the taverns and brothels that most New Town residents preferred not to think about. He was genuinely curious about the life of the people he encountered. It was, he felt, a better education than he could receive at the lectures and classes he should have been attending.

At these Stevenson was infrequently present. When he did attend he scribbled comic verses and sketches at the back of the class, or exchanged whispered comments with fellow-student and lifelong friend Charles Baxter. Finally, in 1871, he told his father that he could not be an engineer; he wanted to be a writer. His father, deeply disappointed but perhaps aware that his son's health was too fragile for the demands of his own profession, consented, on condition that Louis also studied for the Bar, to give himself some solid professional training. Writing was a highly risky business.

The next few years Stevenson spent most of his time in Edinburgh studying law, but at the same time putting himself through an equally rigorous training in the profession of writer. Although he found Edinburgh frustrating, and escaped, especially to France, when he could, the city had a powerful hold on him. He would express a yearning to get away from the sternly Calvinist and hypocritically respectable environment, but he understod the power of the place he had grown up in. Edinburgh had helped to shape his mind and imagination. In *Picturesque Notes* he describes standing on Calton Hill at dusk.

> . . . from all round you there come up the dull hum of the city, the tramp of countless people marching out of time, the rattle of carriages and the continuous keen jingle of the tramway bells. An hour or so before, the gas was turned on; lamplighters scoured the city; in every house, from kitchen to attic, the windows kindled forth into the dusk. And so now, although the town lies blue and darkling on her hills, innumerable spots of the bright element shine far and near along the pavements and upon the facades. Moving lights of the railway pass and repass below the stationary lights upon the bridge. Lights burn in the Jail. Lights burn up in the tall *lands* and on the Castle turrets. They burn low down in the Greenside or along the Park. They run out beyond the other into the dark country. They walk in procession down to Leith, and shine singly far along Leith Pier. Thus, the plan of the city and her suburbs is mapped out upon the ground of blackness, as when a child picks out a drawing full of pinholes and exposes it before a candle; not the darkest night of winter can conceal her high station and

fanciful design; every evening in the year she proceeds to illuminate herself in honour of her own beauty . . .

The pulse of Stevenson's response to his own city, although at times he hated it, would never falter. He adds 'while you are looking, across upon Castle Hill, the drums and bugles begin to recall the scattered garrison; the air thrills with the sound; the bugles sing aloud; and the last rising flourish mounts and melts into the darkness like a star.'

During his years of apprenticeship to the writer's trade, when he practised and imitated and experimented in the ways of putting words together, he was deeply and significantly affected by a number of personal relationships and events. In 1873 he had a drastic confrontation with his parents on the question of religious belief which disturbed him greatly. He could not himself accept conventional Christianity, and his father in particular was shattered by the discovery. For several months argument and hurt prevailed at Heriot Row, and Bob Stevenson was blamed for corrupting the younger Louis. While that was going on Louis met, while visiting a cousin in Suffolk, a man who would help crucially to shape his literary career and a woman who equally crucially affected his emotional life. Sidney Colvin was Slade Professor of Art at Cambridge when Stevenson met him, and was much impressed by the young aspiring writer. He encouraged Louis, helped him to make important contacts with London editors, and criticised his work. Mrs Frances Sitwell, unhappily married and engaged in a longterm platonic relationship with Colvin (they were eventually married), was a beautiful, sensitive and sympathetic woman who was equally taken with the enthusiastic and eager young man whom she met in a Suffolk rectory. Stevenson fell in love with her. She was much older than he was, but for several years he wrote passionate letters to her while at the same time trying to control his feelings for a woman who could never be his. She clearly handled his warmth and impetuosity with sympathetic care.

At that time Stevenson began publishing carefully written essays and shorter pieces in journals and magazines. And he met in Edinburgh a young poet with whom for many years he was to have a stimulating friendship — W.E. Henley. He was helped and couraged not only by Colvin, but by the editor of the *Cornhill Magazine*, the notable literary figure and father of Virginia Woolf, Leslie Stephen. He spent more time in London, getting to know some of the younger writers, amongst whom was Edmund Gosse. Talking, exchanging ideas, and writing, mainly at this time poetry and non-fiction — and letters — were all pursued enthusiastically, although ill-health often interfered and at times he became depressed. It was sometimes hard to believe that he would ever be able to earn a living as a writer.

France offered diversion and stimulus. It was during a visit to an artists' colony at Grez in the Forest of Fontainebleau that Stevenson met the woman who was to become his wife. Fanny Vandegrift Osbourne was an American separated from her husband. She was ten years older than Louis, with an almost grown-up daughter and a younger son, and had come to France to study art. They met in 1876, and for two years Louis spent as much time as possible in France so that he could be near Fanny, in spite of the fact that his parents were very unhappy about the relationship on three counts: Fanny was an American, she was married, and she was much older than he was. In 1878 Fanny had to return to California, and Louis made his famous journey in the Cévennes which he recounted in *Travels With a Donkey*. The previous year his *Inland Voyage* had been published, which described the canoe trip he and his friend Walter Simpson, son of James Young Simpson, had made in Belgium and France the year before.

Louis tolerated separation from Fanny for a year, but in August, 1879, in response to a distuurbing cable from her, he precipitately set forth to join her in California. He had little money and had to travel as cheaply as possible. The trip was arduous and difficult, and nearly killed him. It was after it that he first began to spit blood, and for several months, he was iller than he had ever been before. His parents were devastated. Eventually, after a most demanding period during which Fanny got her divorce, they were married, and Louis's parents reconciled themselves to the idea and welcomed Fanny warmly when they met her. 'I have had a pretty rough time,' Louis wrote to his friend Baxter, 'and God bless my people for coming round when they did, or instead of being able to rest just now, I should have been trying to work and succeeding in

RAIN

THE rain is raining all around,
It falls on field and tree,
It rains on the umbrellas here,
And on the ships at sea.

10

A Child's Garden of Verses

PIRATE·STORY·

THREE of us afloat in the meadow by the
swing,
Three of us aboard in the basket on the lea.
Winds are in the air, they are blowing in the
spring,
And waves are on the meadow like the waves
there are at sea.

Where shall we adventure, to-day that we're afloat,
Wary of the weather and steering by a star?
Shall it be to Africa, a-steering of the boat,
To Providence, or Babylon, or off to Malabar?

11

— dying, I fancy.' His father had undertaken to give them financial help.

The American trip nearly killed Stevenson, but it was productive in many ways. It brought about his marriage to a woman of strong personality, courage and unconventionality, and it brought him experiences which directly affected his writing. While in America he wrote *The Silverado Squatters* and *The Amateur Emigrant*, books in which he confronted his own experiences in a way he had never done before. There were also longterm results. His style became more robust and he began to write fiction again, which he had not done seriously since his adolescence.

Stevenson's health had deteriorated so much that even with the care of Fanny it was no longer possible for him to live in Scotland. The next few years were spent in Switzerland and France, with summer visits to Scotland, but even so life was punctuated by alarming fevers and haemorrhages, and on severl occasions he and Fanny both thought he was dying. He wrote when he could, often in bed, often forcing himself to carry on working when his mind and body resisted the idea. He was determined to make his own way financially, although for many years he was dependent on his father. Without his father's financial support he could never have carried on through the early part of his career, when, although he was praised by many, he could not sell enough books and articles to support an invalid, a wife and a growing stepson.

It was during one of the summer stays in Scotland, at Braemar in 1881, that he wrote the first chapters of the book that would begin to change that — *Treasure Island*. Although not particularly popular when it was serialised in *Young Folks' Magazine* it received much praise when it appeared in book form, and was quickly established as the classic which it has been considered as ever since. In 1885, while living in Bournemouth in the house Stevenson called 'Skerryvore', after the lighthouse built by his uncle Alan Stevenson, he wrote the story that would more dramatically change his fortunes — *The Strange Case of Dr Jekyll and Mr Hyde*. In the same year that was published, 1886, another novel was also produced, which added substantially to Stevenson's reputation. *Kidnapped*, his first novel set in Scotland and wholly involved with Scottish characters, gave Stevenson stature in the eyes of the critics while *Jekyll and Hyde* was a popular success.

While he was living in Bournemouth Stevenson came to know one of the major literary figures of the time who was also perhaps the man who understood him best and with the deepest affection. That man was Henry James, and between them, both in conversation and in print, they discussed some of the most interesting literary ideas of the time. They were particularly concerned with the debate about realism, about whether literature should concentrate on recording reality faithfully in all its unpleasant detail, or whether it should present to the reader an idealised and inspiring picture of the world. Stevenson at that time inclined to the latter opinion, while James argued that it was anyway impossible to represent accurately reality in words. Both over the years would modify their attitudes.

In 1887 Stevenson and his wife returned to the United States. Thomas Stevenson had died, and the money he left his son combined with his growing success as a writer meant that at last Stevenson could fulfil his longings to escape from the confined life at Bournemouth and explore new territory. When he left Edinburgh after his father's funeral he had no idea he was never to return. The city remained vividly in his mind for the rest of his life.

After spending the winter in the Adirondack Mountains, in upper New York State, where Stevenson began to write *The Master of Ballantrae*, they headed west in pursuit of a dream he had been nursing for months. In July, 1888 he and Fanny, accompanied by Louis's mother and Fanny's now grown-up son Lloyd, set sail in a chartered yacht, the *Casco*, for a trip in the Pacific that would take them to the Marquesas, through the Dangerous Archipelago, to Tahiti, and to Hawaii, where in a hut on Waikiki beach Stevenson finished *The Master*.

Those months were not only stimulating to an author who was sharply alive to every fragment of experience, but brought health and an active life to a man who had spent so many years trying to accommodate himself to the dim and constrained life of an invalid. He wrote exultant letters to his friends back home, describing how well and active he was, how he was swimming and walking and riding, and working hard too. The experience was in every way good for him, psychologically and physically. 'The cruise has been a great success,' he wrote to Baxter from Honolulu, 'both as to matter, fun, and health.' He even relished the storms and the moments when they were in real danger: 'we don't mind squalls any longer, and eh, man, that's a great thing'. But for Fanny the experience was less positive. She was a poor sailor, and not young, and although she had considerable talent for roughing it the trip was at times a strain for her.

After a prolonged stay in Hawaii the Stevenson party, now without Stevenson's mother, continued their South Sea explorations, aboard the *Equator*, which was trading in the islands. That trip took them to the Gilberts and finally to Samoa. It was a voyage of much educational value for Stevenson. He learned about trading in the South Seas, about the economic relations between natives and whites, about exploitation, all of which would feed his fiction. On board the *Equator* in collaboration with Lloyd Osbourne he began to write *The Wrecker*. Within days of landfall at Apia in Samoa Stevenson became the owner of the tract of land that was to become his final home. He had proved beyond doubt that the South Pacific allowed him to live and operate in a way that he had not experienced for years. Although at that stage he still intended to return for a while to Britain (a spell of severe illness in Sydney finally put an end to that idea) the advantages of making a permanent home on the other side of the world were irresistible. Friends at home were appalled at the idea. Henry James was one of the few who recognised how important it was for Stevenson to be liberated from the constraints of invalidism.

Louis and Fanny Stevenson left Apia leaving instructions about clearing the land and building a house, to be called Vailima. They went to Australia, thinking it was the first leg of a journey home. In deciding to make Samoa his permanent home, factors were involved other than the question of health, though that was crucial. He would still have periods of ill-health, but for much of the time he could experience the exhilaration of being able to lead the kind of life that had always attracted him. As well as that, he had become intensely interested in the life and politics of the South Pacific. He wanted to write about both, much to the consternation of those at home like Colvin, who saw his future as a writer in continuing to produce pleasing adventure stories, possibly drawing on Scotland's history. Stevenson was witnessing at first hand aspects of colonialism and exploitation that had rarely been discussed. He had learned about the culture of a people whom he found very attractive. Those who had written about the Pacific had emphasised the romance of the islands, the charm of the people, the appeal of ocean and sunshine and plenty. On the *Casco* and *Equator* trips, and on his later trip on the little freighter *Janet Nichol*, Stevenson explored, as he had done years before in Edinburgh, the underside of the picturesque view. He was determined to write about what he observed.

In *A Footnote to History* he wrote about the political situation of Samoa, and the way in which the rivalry between three major powers, Germany, America and Britain, had fragmented her people and her dignity. He wrote lengthy letters to Sidney Colvin (which Colvin criticised for being too full of what he considered to be tedious detail about the lives and concerns of the

Cummy Reading

islanders), and he also wrote to *The Times*. And he wrote fiction. The best known of the Pacific stories, *The Wrecker* is also his weakest, although there are some splendid passages. In *The Beach of Falesá* and *The Ebb-Tide*, he wrote two striking stories about the European presence in the Pacific islands. Stevenson knew that in both he had caught something of the truth about the islands.

Vailima was hard work. Fanny and Louis were aiming to produce enough on the estate to be at least self-sufficient, but they ran into all kinds of problems. Yet Stevenson was well enough to do his share of the planting and weeding as well as to carry on with his writing. He wrote to his publisher in New York, 'my hands are covered with blisters and full of thorns; letters are, doubtless, fine things, so are beer and skittles, but give me farmering in the tropics for real interest'. The house they built was expensive, and expensively equipped. Stevenson referred to it wryly as his 'Subpriorsford', echoing Sir Walter Scott's Abbotsford which had been partly responsible for that great writer's financial ruin. By this time Stevenson also had a large extended family to provide for. Although he had no children of his own, there were Fanny's two, Lloyd and Belle, and for a time Belle's husband Joe Strong, and their son Austin, and the elder Mrs Stevenson also joined them later. Louis was genuinely fond of Lloyd, Belle and Austin, but Joe Strong was an embarrassing burden until he and Belle separated. And all of them were a drain on his financial and emotional resources.

In those last years Stevenson was full of ideas for books and although there were depressing periods when he found it impossible to write and the problems and anxieties concerning Vailima and those in his care multiplied, his imagination never became sterile. Fanny's health deteriorated, which was an intense worry for him, although he was reluctant to admit to his friends and correspondents how bad it really was. She was for a time mentally unstable, but Stevenson had coped with difficulties all his life, had written under the most adverse circumstances, and had maintained his positive outlook on life, his sense of humour, and his high spirits. He was able to conquer depression and anxiety partly through a thoroughly professional attitude to his writing. He had never been the kind of writer to wait for inspiration before he put pen to paper. Writing was a job that had to be done, just like any other job, and had always to be done to the best of his ability.

When Stevenson died at Vailima, on 3 December, 1894, he was engaged in working on a number of projects based on his Scottish background. One, *Weir of Hermiston*, is often thought of as his finest work. His imagination seemed to thrive on distance, and his ear seemed more finely attuned to the rich speech of his past life. His South Seas experiences added substance to both the style and content of his work. He gained courage and direction

R.L.S. aged 2, with his mother

in the way he approached his subjects, whether Scottish or Pacific. He had needed, perhaps, not only new experiences, but the distance both from Scotland and the London literary scene, which was in its way as inhibiting as his Calvinist upbringing.

On the day he died Stevenson had been busy on *Weir of Hermiston*. At the end of a satisfactory day's writing he went down to join Fanny, and it was while the two of them were preparing their evening meal that he suddenly collapsed. It was not his lungs that killed him, but a cerebral haemorrhage, probably caused by the accumulation of strain and anxiety. The immediate family, the Samoans who worked at Vailima, everyone who had ever come into contact with him and many who had only read him, were stricken. He was buried on the top of Mt Vaea, that rose behind Vailima.

All the pieces in this collection were written when the memory of Robert Louis Stevenson was still vivid. The reputation that he left behind him was affected considerably by sentimentality in the years immediately following his death. His personal charm, the engaging nature of much of his writing, and the fact that he had died young in a romantic part of the world, all contributed to it. His first biographer, a cousin, Graham Balfour, who had visited him at Vailima, had a difficult job, for he, and those whose cooperation was essential for the biography, were very reluctant to record anything that might damage Louis's popularity, or the innocent appeal of his reputation. The public was eager to preserve a golden image of Stevenson, and those who had been closest were very anxious not to sully this. It was in reaction to that kind of attitude, which he felt pervaded Graham Balfour's biography, that W.E. Henley wrote his notorious 'Seraph in Chocolate' piece for the *Pall Mall Magazine*, which is reproduced here. He had shared with Stevenson many of his less reputable escapades, explored the backstreets and the brothels of Edinburgh with him, and exchanged rebellious and irreverent ideas. The Stevenson he wanted to capture for was the wild, independent young man, but he forgot that even at his most rebellious Stevenson never lost a strong moral feeling, a deep-rooted if unconventional sense of responsibility to humanity. Henley's article is coloured also by the fact that he and Stevenson had quarrelled painfully in 1888, and neither had ever really got over it. Henley believed that Stevenson had compromised himself and his principles in the process of becoming a popular writer.

The articles by Sidney Colvin and Edmund Gosse happily remember the man of spontaneity and charm and fine feeling. Colvin had been invaluable to Stevenson's career, advising him and smoothing his way initially. When Stevenson was abroad Colvin acted, in conjunction with Charles Baxter in Edinburgh, as agent and editor. He loved Stevenson, and cared profoundly about his work. Yet it is arguable that his influence was not altogether for the best. He was conventional, overanxious about public reaction; he disliked both *The Ebb-Tide* and *The Beach of Falesá* because he considered them unpleasantly realistic. Both he and Gosse were convinced that it was fatal for Stevenson to be so far away from what they considered to be the literary centre of the world — London. Gosse, just a year older than Stevenson, had perhaps a more companionable and more lively understanding of the man. He wrote his piece very soon after Stevenson's death.

Of all Stevenson's friends the man who was most intimately attuned to his endeavours as man and writer was certainly Henry James. He hoped passionately that Stevenson would become one of the great writers of the last quarter of the century, and everything he wrote about him is underlined by this generous attitude. The piece included here was written on the publication of Stevenson's letters, edited by Colvin. The James and Stevenson friendship was one of *the* literary relationships of the period.

Will Low was an American painter and a close friend particularly of the years before Stevenson's marriage. He shared many of Stevenson's adventures in France, and also knew Bob Stevenson well. His autobiographical book *Chronicle of Friendships* is much concerned with Louis and Bob, and the piece included here is an extract from it. He gives a vivid picture of the young cousins in Paris and Fountainebleu, exploring life and ideas, eccentric, spirited. Low came to know Stevenson well, but J.M. Barrie only encountered him once, on that occasion when he was transported away from his university class to Rutherford's bar. They corresponded when Stevenson was in Samoa, and he was for Barrie, as for a number of young Scottish writers at the time, the most creative figure of a slightly older generation. The article reproduced here was written before Stevenson had written his best work, but it shows how he had already been identified as a man who could raise fiction to the highest level.

In each of the articles in this collection the sense of Stevenson's attractiveness as man and writer is powerful. The attractiveness both made and undid his reputation. It meant that, once the first burst of grief and regret and remembrance was over, his real achievement was forgotten, or lost in a vague and sentimental awareness that he was a splendid writer of fairly undemanding stories and poems. He should be remembered for that impact he made as man and writer on his contemporaries; but he should be remembered also — as all those who are included here were aware — as a man who, in what he was, what he did, and what he wrote, demonstrated 'a spirit itense and rare', the reaction of a sensitive and questing mind to the challenge of an economically successful society in search of the imagination.

Robert Louis Stevenson

SIDNEY COLVIN

Readers and lovers of Stevenson, in my experience, are generally to be divided into two sorts or classes. One sort care most for his stories, delighting in the humorous or tragic vitality of his characters and the thrill of the situations in which he puts them. The other sort are more interested in the man himself, and prefer the essays and letters, the books of travel and reminiscence in which he takes you into his own company and confidence. Readers of this latter class would rather paddle with Stevenson in his canoe down the Sambre and Oise, look out with him from the tower of Noyon Cathedral, or join in his farewell greetings to the three Graces of Origny — they would rather sleep under the stars with him and the she-ass Modestine in the woods of Gévaudan, or hear him moralize on the life of the Trappist monks in the convent of Our Lady of the Snows — than they would crouch in the apple-barrel with Jim Hawkins on board *Hispaniola* and overhear the plotting of the mutineers, or lie sick with David Balfour in the house of Robin Oig while the host and Alan Breck challenge each other to their match upon the pipes. It pleases such readers better to learn from Stevenson in the first person how his Brownies, as he calls them, furnished to him in dreams the most shudderful incidents in the parable of Jekyll and Hyde than to read these incidents themselves in the pages of the book. The fortunes of Prince Otto and Seraphina and Gondremark and Countess von Rosen interest them, it may be, less in the tale itself than in the letters in which Stevenson tells his correspondents of his delightful toil over the tale and of the high hopes that he has built upon it. They may be less moved — though that I find it hard to conceive — by the scene of the torn hymn-book and the birth of passion between Archie Weir and Kirstie Eliot in the little Pentland church than by the note of acute personal emotion which a thought of the same church arouses in Stevenson writing to a friend from exile.[1]

My own view is that both sides of him — the creative artist and the human personality — are interesting and admirable alike. But what I am now about to write will concern the man himself rather than any phase of his work. I shall dip a random bucket into the well of memory, and try whether the yield, from our fourteen years of close intimacy, may be such as to supplement and complete to any purpose the image which readers may otherwise have formed of him. And first, to wipe away some false impressions which seem to be current: I lately found one writer, because Stevenson was thin, speaking of him as having been a "shadowy" figure; another, because he was an invalid, describing him as "anaemic," and a third as "thin-blooded." Shadowy! he was indeed all his life a bag of bones, a very lath for leanness; as lean as Shakespeare's Master Slender, or let us say as Don Quixote. Nevertheless when he was in the room it was the other people, and not he, who seemed the shadows. The most robust and ordinary men seemed to turn dim and null in presence of the vitality that glowed in the steadfast, penetrating fire of the lean man's eyes, the rich, compelling charm of his smile, the lissom swiftness of his movements and lively expressiveness of his gestures, above all in the irresistible sympathetic play and abundance of his talk. Anaemic! thin-blooded! the main physical fact about him, according to those of his doctors whom I have questioned, was that his heart was too big and its blood supply too full for his body. There was failure of nutrition, in the sense that he could never make flesh; there was weakness of the throat and lungs, weakness above all of the arteries, never of the heart itself, nor did his looks, even in mortal illness and exhaustion, ever give the impression of bloodlessness. More than one

1.   Colvin is in error here, a misapprehension he shares with a number of readers of *Weir of Hermiston*. Archie meets Kirstie in the Borders, in Elliot (Colvin has the spelling wrong) country, at a considerable distance from Edinburgh. Stevenson borrowed the placenames 'Hermiston' and 'Cauldstaneslap' from the Pentlands, very close to Edinburgh, and transposed them. Archie is banished to Hermiston. It would make little sense if he had been sent only a few miles from the city.

of his early friends, in describing him as habitually pale, have let their memory be betrayed by knowledge of what might have been expected in one so frail in health. To add, as some have done, that his hair was black is to misdescribe him still farther. As a matter of fact his face, forehead and all, was throughout the years when I knew him of an even, rather high, colour varying little whether he was ill or well; and his hair, of a lightish brown in youth, although the brown grew darker with years, and darker still, I believe, in the tropics, can never have approached black.

If you want to realize the kind of effect he made, at least in the early years when I knew him best, imagine this attenuated but extraordinarily vivid and vital presence, with something about it that at first struck you as freakish, rare, fantastic, a touch of the elfin and unearthly, a sprite, an Ariel. And imagine that, as you got to know him, this sprite, this visitant from another sphere, turned out to differ from mankind in general not by being less human but by being a great deal more human than they; richer-blooded, greater-hearted; more human in all senses of the word, for he comprised within himself, and would flash on you in the course of a single afternoon, all the different ages and half the different characters of man, the unfaded freshness of a child, the ardent outlook and adventurous day-dreams of a boy, the steadfast courage of manhood, the quick sympathetic tenderness of a woman, and already, as early as the mid-twenties of his life, an almost uncanny share of the ripe life-wisdom of old age. He was a fellow of infinite and unrestrained jest and yet of infinite earnest, the one very often a mask for the other; a poet, an artist, an adventurer; a man beset with fleshly frailties, and despite his infirm health of strong appetites and unchecked curiosities; and yet a profoundly sincere moralist and preacher and son of the Covenanters after his fashion, deeply conscious of the war within his members, and deeply bent on acting up to the best he knew. Henley tried to sum him up in a well-known sonnet:

Thin-legged, thin-chested, slight unspeakably,
Neat-footed and weak-fingered: in his face —
Lean, large-boned, curved of beak, and touched with race,
Bold-lipped, rich-tinted, mutable as the sea,
The brown eyes radiant with vivacity —
There shines a brilliant and romantic grace,

A spirit intense and rare, with trace on trace
Of passion and impudence and energy.
Valiant in velvet, light in ragged luck,
Most vain, most generous, sternly critical,
Buffoon and poet, lover and sensualist:
A deal of Ariel, just a streak of Puck,
Much Anthony, of Hamlet most of all,
And something of the Shorter-Catechist.

In that sonnet Henley has drawn up a lively and showy — or shall we not rather say flashy? — enough catalogue of the diverse qualities and contradictory aspects which he recognized in his friend. But the pity is that as there described those qualities lie like spillikins, unrelated and disconnected. Henley has missed what gave its unity to the character and what every other among his nearer friends soon discovered to be the one essential, never failing and ever endearing thing under all that play and diversity of being. This was the infinitely kind and tender, devotedly generous, brave and loving heart of the man.

I first saw him at the beginning of August, 1873, that is all but forty-eight years ago, when he was twenty-three and I twenty-eight. I had landed from a Great-Eastern train at a little country station in Suffolk, and was met on the platform by a stripling in a velvet jacket and straw hat, who walked up with me to the country rectory where he was staying and where I had come to stay. I had lately been appointed Slade Professor at Cambridge; the rectory was that of Cockfield, near Bury St. Edmunds; the host was my much older colleague Professor Churchill Babington, of amiable and learned memory; the hostess was his wife, a grand-daughter of the Rev. Lewis Balfour of Colinton, Midlothian; the youth was her young first cousin by the mother's side, Louis Stevenson from Edinburgh. The first shyness over I realized in the course of that short walk how well I had done to follow the advice of a fellow-guest who had preceded me in the house — to wit Mrs Sitwell, my wife as she came later on to be. She had written to me about this youth, declaring that I should find him a real young genius and urging me to come if I could before he went away. I could not wonder at what I presently learnt — how within an hour of his first appearance at the rectory, knapsack on back, a few days earlier, he had captivated the whole household. To his cousin the hostess, a woman of a fine sympathetic nature and quick, humorous intelligence, he was of course well known beforehand, though she had never seen him in so charming a light as now. With her husband the Professor, a clergyman of solid antiquarian and ecclesiastical knowledge and an almost Pickwickian simplicity of character corresponding to his lovable rotund visage and innocently beaming spectacles — with the Professor, "Stivvy," as he called his wife's young cousin, was already something of a favourite. Of their guests, I found one, a boy of ten, watching for every moment when he could monopolize the newcomer's attention, either to show off to him the scenes of his toy theatre or to conduct him confidentially by the hand about the garden or beside the moat; while between him and the boy's mother, Mrs Sitwell, there had sprung up an instantaneous understanding. Not only the lights and brilliancies of his nature, but the strengths and glooms that underlay them, were from the first apparent to her, so that in the trying season of his life which followed he was moved to throw himself upon her sympathies with the unlimited confidence and devotion to which his letters of the time bear witness. He sped those summer nights and days for us all as I have scarce known any sped before or since. He seemed, this youngster, already to have lived and seen and felt and dreamed and laughed and longed more than others do in a lifetime. He showed himself moreover full of reading, at least in English and French — for his Latin was shaky and Greek he only got at through translations. Over wide ranges of life and letters his mind and speech ran like the fingers of a musician over the keyboard of an instrument. Pure poetic eloquence (coloured always, be it remembered, by a strong Scottish accent), grave argument and criticism, riotous freaks of fancy, flashes of nonsense more illuminating than wisdom, streamed from him inexhaustibly as he kindled with delight at the delight of his hearers.

Strange to say, this brilliant creature, though he had made one or two close and appreciative intimates of his own age and sex, had not been thought good enough for the polite society of his native Edinburgh. In most of the few houses which he frequented he seems to have been taken for an eccentric and affected kind of Bohemian *poseur*, to be treated at best with toleration. In a book, or if I remember rightly in more than one book, on his early Edinburgh days, a member of one of those houses, and

Thomas Stevenson and R.L.S., 1866

sister of one of his special friends, has since his death written of him in a fine superior tone of retrospective condescension. In new and more sympathetic company his social genius immediately expanded and glowed as I have said, till all of us seemed to catch something of his own gift and inspiration. This power of inspiring others has been noted by many of those who knew Stevenson later as an especial and distinguishing mark of his conversation. As long as he was there you kept discovering with delight unexpected powers in yourself. You felt as if you had taken service with a conjuror, whom you supplied with balls of clay and who took them and turned them into gold and sent them whirling and glowing about his head, making you believe all the while that they were still truly yours.

But on further acquaintance it soon became clear that under all this captivating, this contagious gaiety and charm there lay a troubled spirit, in grave risk from the perils of youth, from a constitution naturally frail and already heavily over-strained, from self-distrust and uncertainty as to his own powers and purposes, and above all from the misery of bitter, heart- and soul-rending disagreements with a father to whom he was devotedly attached. It was only when, after a brief return to Edinburgh from Cockfield, he came south again in the next month that we discovered so much concerning him. He spent his time partly in London and partly with me in a cottage I then inhabited in the southern hill-suburb of Norwood. With various types of genius and of the charm and power of genius among my elders I had already, as indicated in some of the earlier pages of this book, had fortunate opportunities of becoming familiar. In this brilliant and troubled Scotch youth I could not fail to realize that here, among my juniors, was a genius who might well fail on the threshold of life, but who, if he could only win through, had it in him to take as shining a place as any of them. No wonder if we, his new friends, were keen to do all we could for him in the way of help and sympathy. It was no surprise to us when towards mid-October, after a second return to Edinburgh, his letters brought news of threatening illness, now when, having again come south to be examined, as had been agreed with his father, for admission into one of the London Inns of Court, he had perforce to change his purpose and undergo a different kind of examination at the hands of Sir Andrew Clark. That wise physician peremptorily ordered him a period of rest in the soothing climate of the French Riviera, out of reach of all occasion or possibility of contention with those he loved at home.

The recollections of him that remain with me from the next few years are partly of two visits I paid him in the course of that first winter (1873-1874) on the Riviera; partly of visits he paid me in the Norwood cottage, or in another cottage I rented a little later at Hampstead, or later again in college rooms which I occupied as a professor at Cambridge; partly from his various descents upon or passages through London, made sometimes from Edinburgh and sometimes from France, after his return in 1874 to his now reconciled home. The points in his character these stray recollections chiefly illustrate are, first, the longing for a life of action and adventure, which in an ordinary youth might have passed as a matter of course but in one already so stricken in health seemed pathetically vain; next, his inborn faculty — a very much rarer gift — as an artist in letters, and the scrupulous self-training by which almost from boyhood he had been privately disciplining it: then the intensely, quite exceptionally, observing and loving interest he took in young children: and above all, that magical power he had of winning the delighted affection, the immediate confidence, of men and women of the most various sorts and conditions, always excepting those hide-bound in starched propriety or conventional officialdom, whom he had a scare less unfailing power of putting against him at first sight.

At the Suffolk rectory he had been neatly enough clad: most of the images of him that rise next before me present him in the slovenly, nondescript Bohemian garments and untrimmed hair which it was in those days his custom to wear. I could somehow never feel this to be an affectation in Stevenson, or dislike it as I should have been apt to dislike and perhaps despise it in anybody else. We agree to give the name of affectation to anything markedly different from common usage in little, every-day outward things — unconcerning things, as the poet Donne calls them. But affectation is affectation indeed only when a person does or says that which is false to his or her nature. And given a nature differing sufficiently from the average, perhaps the real affectation would be that it should force itself to preserve an average outside to the world. Stevenson's uncut hair came originally from the fear of catching cold. His shabby clothes came partly from lack of cash, partly from lack of care, partly, as I think I have said elsewhere, from a hankering after social experiment and

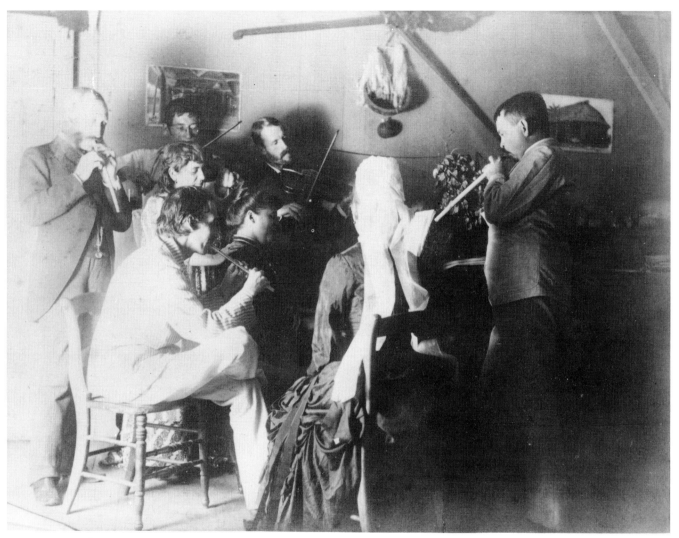

Musical group, Casco

adventure, and a dislike of being identified with any special class or caste. Certainly conventional and respectable attire, when by exception he wore it, did not in those days sit him well. Going with me one day from Hampstead to the Royal Academy Exhibition, he thought such attire would be expected of him, and looked out a black frock coat and tall hat which he had once worn at a wedding. I can see now the odd figure he made as he walked with me in that unwonted garb down Regent Street and along Piccadilly. True, he carried his tall hat not on his head, but in his hand because it chafed him. Also, being fresh from an enthusiastic study of the prosody of Milton, he kept declaiming to me with rapturous comments as we walked the lines and cadences which chiefly haunted him:

"His wrath
Burned after them to the bottomless pit."
"Like Teneriffe or Atlas, unremoved—"
"All night the dreadless angel, unpursued —"
"Oh! how comely it is and how reviving
To the spirits of just men long opprest!"

It was while he declaimed these last two lines, the opening of a famous chorus in *Sampson Agonistes*, that the gates of Burlington House, I remember, enfolded us.

Most characteristic of his ordinary ways was his appearance one very early morning from London at the Norwood cottage. He presented himself to my astonished servant, on her opening the shutters, wearing a worn-out sleeved waistcoat over a black flannel shirt, and weary and dirty from a night's walking followed by a couple of hours' slumber in a garden outhouse he had found open. He had spent the night on the pad through the southern slums and suburbs, trying to arouse the suspicions of one policeman after another till he should succeed in getting taken up as a rogue and vagabond and thereby gaining proof for his fixed belief that justice, at least in the hands of its subordinate officers, has one pair of scales for the ragged and another for the respectable. But one and all saw through him, and refused to take him seriously as a member of the criminal classes. Though surprised at their penetration, and rather crestfallen at the failure of his attempt, he had had his reward in a number of friendly and entertaining conversations with the members of the force, ending generally in confidential disclosures as to their private affairs and feelings.

Foreign officials and police, not to speak of *attachés* and bank clerks and managers, were not so clear-sighted, and he sometimes came in for worse treatment than he bargained for. Readers remember, I dare say, his account of his expulsion by the hostess of La Fère in the *Inland Voyage*, still more that of his arrest and temporary imprisonment by the Commissary of Police at Châtillon-sur-Loing, which is one of the most delectable pieces of humorous narrative in English literature. Troubles of this kind had their consolation in that they gave him matter for the entertainment of his readers. Not so the rebuffs he sometimes underwent when he visited embassies or banks on business concerned with passports or letters of credit. I have known him made actually ill by futile anger at the contumelious reception he met with in such places. He lacked the power, which comes only too naturally from most men sprung, as he was, from a stock accustomed to command, of putting down insolence by greater insolence. He could rage, indeed, but usually his rage was ineffectual and only brought a dangerous rush of blood to his head and eyes. Once, however, he had his revenge and his hour of triumph, of which to my deep regret I was not myself a witness. On the way from Nice to Royat he had stopped at Clermont-Ferrand, the old provincial capital of Auvergne. He went to a bank to cash some circular notes of the British Linen Company in Edinburgh. His appearance had the usual, almost magical, effect of arousing in the business mind suspicions, amounting to conviction, of his dishonesty. The men in office roundly told him that there was no such firm among their correspondents; that they more than suspected him of having come with intent to defraud, but as an act of kindness would give him five minutes to make himself scarce before they sent for the police. For once he kept his head and temper, outwardly at least; sturdily declined to leave the premises; and insisted that the police should be sent for immediately. Presently his eye was caught by a rack of pigeon-holes containing letters and documents which by some intuition he saw or divined to be from foreign correspondents of the firm; dashed at it despite all remonstrances; rummaged the papers before the eyes of the astonished clerks; drew forth in triumph a bundle containing correspondence from the British Linen Company, including the letter of credit for himself; demanded that the partners and men in authority should be brought down, and when they appeared, exposed to them with a torrent of scornful eloquence their misconduct of their business, and drew a terrifying picture of the ruin that they must inevitably reap from such treatment of distinguished foreign clients. His triumph was complete: the whole house, partners and clerks, abased themselves in regrets and apologies, and escorted him to the door

The *Janet Nicol*

with fawning demonstrations of respect. This was his day of victory; *strages bankeroroum* he called it, and went off and at once designed a medal — never, I believe, executed — in its commemoration.

But this story belongs to a later date; and to go back to my own memories of the early days — I went twice to see him during that invalid winter on the Riviera. He had been staying at Mentone (I should properly say Menton, but those of us who remember the place before the annexation of Savoy and Nice to France cannot bring ourselves to spell or pronounce it except in the more euphonious Italian manner). I proposed that he should move to meet me as far (some six miles) as Monaco); the aspect of that tiny capital, with the exquisite capricous charm of its situation on a high peninsular rock between the harbour and the outer sea, having strongly caught my fancy as a boy in driving along the Corniche road with my father, and made me desire to explore it from within. There we accordingly spent four or five days, and then four or five more in one of the quiter hotels at Monte Carlo. My memories of the time have merged for the most part into a generalized impression of sunlit hours spent basking in a row-boat about the bay, and sped by endless talk which ran forward beyond the present days of illness to ardent schemes both of literature and adventure, the one as vividly imagined and worded as the other. Stevenson has brought home to the senses of his readers, by a magical phrase or two, the pungently delicious mingled scent of pine and juniper and myrtle and rosemary which in sunny weather comes wafted from the Cap Martin over the shoreward waters of that sea: he revelled in this scent, and I believe it was already carrying him in imagination on voyages to far-off spice-islands of the East. Of the literary projects broached between us the only one I remember was a spectacle-play on that transcendent type of human vanity, Herostratus, who to keep his name from being forgotten kindled the fire that burned down the temple of Ephesus. Psychology and scenic effects as Stevenson descanted on them come up together in my memory even yet, not in any exactness of detail, but only in a kind of vague dazzle and flamboyance.

There was one sort of excitement and one form of risk which at no time had any lure for Louis and which he hated alike by instinct and principle, and into that famous and fascinating cosmopolitan hell, the Casino of Monte Carlo, he never entered. Once or twice I looked in by myself to watch the play; and the last time, hearing a sudden sharp "ping" from near the wall of the room over my right shoulder, I turned and saw that a loser having left the table lay writhing on the floor. He had shot himself, fatally as I afterwards learnt, in the stomach. The attendants promptly came forward, lifted him on to an armchair, and carried him out of the room with an air of grave disapproval and shocked decorum. When I told Louis of the scene he took a disgust at the place, and we left it together for Mentone. After I had seen him installed in fresh and comfortable quarters in the Hotel Mirabeau, now defunct, at the eastern end of the town, I left for Paris, where I had a few weeks' work to do. Returning in January, I found him enjoying the company of two Russian sisters living in a villa annexed to the hotel, ladies some twenty years older than himself, to whom and to their children he had become quickly and warmly attached. I say their children, for we never could make out which child belonged to which sister, or whether one of the two was not the mother of them both. Both were brilliantly accomplished and cultivated women, one having all the unblushing outspokenness of her race, its unchecked vehemence and mutability in mirth and anger, in scorn, attachment, or aversion; the other much of an invalid, consistently gentle and sympathetic, and withal an exquisite musician. For Stevenson this sister conceived a great quasi-maternal tenderness, and one of the odd tricks of memory has played me is that my nerves retain even now the sense of her sharp twitch of pain as I spoke one day, while she was walking with her arm in mine, of the fears entertained by his friends for his health and future. It was the younger of the two children who figures so much under her name Nelitchka in his letters of the time. Hardly any one has written of young children with such yearning inwardness of love combined with so analytic intentness and subtlety of observation as he. But how, the reader may interrupt, how about the illustrious Victor Hugo with his *L'Art d'être grand-père* and his *Les Enfants*? The comparison indeed sounds crushing; but perhaps Hugo's work in this kind, full of genius as it is, full of insight and tenderness, would impress more if there were not so overwhelmingly much of it, if it did not burden us with a sense of almost mechanical abundance and redundance and iteration. The small objects of Stevenson's passionately delighted study were not always at first won or attracted by him. Rather they were apt to feel discomposed under the intensity of the beaming gaze he fastened upon them; and it was with a touch of womanly affront at feeling herself too hard stared at that the baby Nelichka (aged two and a half) addressed him by a word for "rogue" or "naughty man" she had lately picked up in Italy, "Berecchino!" Parental interposition presently reconciled her, and they became fast friends and playmates; but the name stuck, and for Nellie, throughout those weeks when the child's company and the watching of her indefatigable tottering efforts to dance, and dance, and dance to her mother's music were among his chief delights — for Nellie, Stevenson was never anything but Monsieur Berecchino. But of this more anon.

Another memory of the time illustrates the hopeless incompatibility that existed between this young genius and the more frozen types of bourgeois conventionality. There was at our hotel a young or youngish, well-groomed Frenchman of this class, the quintessence of respectable nullity and complacent correctness, who sat at the same long table with us for some weeks. At our end of the table, besides Stevenson and myself with the Russian ladies and their children, there sat also a bearded French landscape painter, Robinet by name, in opinions a violent clerical and reactionary, but an artist and the best of genial good fellows. Day after day Stevenson kept this little company in an enchanted atmosphere of mirth and mutual delight with one another and with him. But the glow which enkindled the rest of us stopped dead short of the correct Frenchman, who sat a little apart, icily isolated, annoyed, envying, disapproving. Stevenson, I think, was hardly aware of his existence at all, more than of a wooden dummy. R.L.S. was drawing more or less consciously from himself when he wrote of one of his characters, Dick Naseby in *The Story of a Lie* — He was a type-hunter among mankind. He despised small game and insignificant personalities, where in the shape of dukes or bagmen, letting them go by like seaweed; but show him a refined or powerful face, let him hear a plangent or a penetrating voice, fish for him with a living look in some one's eye, a passionate gesture, a meaning or ambiguous smile, and his mind was instantaneously awakened. Finding himself thus left out in the cold, not rudely or on purpose, for Stevenson was incapable of a conscious rudeness, but nevertheless left out, from a company which included obviously attractive ladies, my Frenchman could not bear it. One day, on the occasion of some commonplace civility I showed him, he confided to me, with no breach of correct manners, the extreme distaste and resentment he had conceived against my friend, and even dictated that he

would like to call him out if he could find an excuse. There was nothing to be done, no possible point of mutual contact or understanding between them. I could but affably suggest that he would be likely to find more sympathetic company at another hotel; and he took the hint.

The warm regard which sprang up in these Mentone days between Stevenson and those two Russian sisters led to a promise that in the next summer he should pay them a visit in their own country. But circumstances made it impossible for him to fulfil the promise; the intimacy of those winter months on the Riviera had no sequel save a correspondence which flagged after a few months and by and by failed altogether; and nether he nor I ever saw or heard of either sister again.

To the same winter months of the French Riviera belongs the first meeting of Stevenson with another gifted Scotsman of letters, Andrew Lang, in those days also threatened with lung trouble, who became his friend and long outlived him. It seems indeed but the other day that we had to mourn the loss from among us of that kind, learned, whimsical, many-faceted character — scholar, critic, poet, journalist, folk-lorist, humanist, and humorist; and in the mind's eye of many of us there still lives freshly the aspect of the half-silvered hair setting off the all but black eyebrows and gipsy eyes; of the chiselled features, the smiling languid face and grace behind which there lurked intellectual energies so keen and varied, accomplishments so high, so insatiable a spirit of curiosity and research under a guise so airy and playful. A fault, or flaw, or perversity in Lang, no doubt, was the trick of flippancy which he allowed to spoil some of his work and which masked altogether from some eyes the fine substance and quality of the man. Another was the habitual preoccupation with his own ideas which made his manner, to women especially, often seen careless and abstracted, or even rude, when rudeness was farthest from his intention. But towards his friends there was no man steadier in kindness or more generous in appreciation, as I for one can testify from more than forty years experience, and as Stevenson had full occasion to know. It was not without some trepidation that I first brought them together in those Mentone days, for I suppose no two young Scots, especially no two sharing so many literary tastes, were ever more unlike by temperament and training. On the one hand the young Oxford don, a successful and typical scholar on the regular academic lines, picturesque by the gift of nature but fastidiously correct and reserved, purely English in speech, with a recurring falsetto note in the voice — that kind of falsetto that bespeaks languor rather than vehemence, full of literature and pleasantry but on his guard even to affectation, against any show of emotion, and consitently dissembling the *perfervidum ingenium* of his race, if he had it, under a cloak of indifference and light banter. On the other hand the brilliant, irregularly educated lad from Edinburgh, to the conventional eye an eccentrically ill-clad and long-haired nondescript, with the rich Lallan accent on his tongue, the obvious innate virility and spirit of adventure in him even in mutiny against the invalid habits imposed by ill-health, the vivid, demonstrative ways, every impulse of his heart and mind flashing out in the play of eye, feature, and gesture no less than in the humorous riot and poetical abundance of his talk. There were symptoms during, and even after, the first meeting of the two which seemed as though the kind of misunderstanding might spring up between them which I had feared; but such an immediate result having been happily averted they learned quickly to appreciate each other's gifts and company, and remained fast friends to the end. There are few finer tributes by one man of letters to another, his contemporary, than that of Lang to Stevenson in the introduction to the Swanston edition.

After his return from the Riviera in 1874 Stevenson was elected to the Savile club, then quartered in the house in Savile Row from which it takes its name and which it afterwards outgrew. (It had previously led for a few years a precarious kind of chrysalis existence, under the title of the New Club, in Spring Gardens off Charing Cross.) This little society had been founded on a principle aimed against the standoffishness customary in English club life, and all members were expected to hold themselves predisposed to talk and liable to accost without introduction. Stevenson's earliest friends in the club besides myself were Fleeming Jenkin, the most versatile and vivacious, most pugnaciously minded and friendliest-hearted of men the single one among his Edinburgh seniors and teachers who had seen what the lad was worth, truant

pupil though he might be, and made a friend of him; and my Cambridge contemporary, Professor W.K. Clifford, that short-lived genious unequalled and unapproached, as those aver who can follow him, in the rarefied region of specualtion where the higher mathematics and metaphysics merge into one. In spheres of thought and study more accessible to the rest of us, Clifford had a beautiful lucidity of mind and mastery of style, and in ordinary human intercourse was extremely striking and attractive, with his powerful head and blunt Socratic features, the candid, almost childlike, upcast look of his light grey-blue eyes between their dark lashes, the tripping and easy, again almost childlike, simplicity of speech and manner with which he would debate the profoundest problems, and the quite childlike pleasure he took in all manner of fun and nonsense and surprises and fairy-tales (I leave out his freaks of prowess and daring as an athlete and a dozen of his other claims to regard and admiration). That such a man, having met Stevenson once or twice in my company, should be keen to back him for the club was a matter of course. Nor did the members in general, being for the most part young men drawn from the professions of science or learning, of art, literature, journalism, or the stage, fail to appreciate the new-comer. On his visits to London he generally lunched there, and at the meal and afterwards came to be accepted and habitually surrounded as a radiating centre of good talk, a kind of ideal incarnation of the spirit of the society. Comparatively rare as they were, I believe that both his presences in those days and his tradition subsequently contributed as much as anything towards the success and prosperity of the club. Mr Edmund Gosse, who joined us a couple of years later, had given a pleasantly vivid picture of the days when an introduction at the Savile, renewing the memory of a chance meeting on a Highland pleasure-steamer six years before, laid the foundations of his and Stevenson's friendship. One signal case of failure remains indeed in some of our memories. A certain newly elected member of some social and literary standing, but unacquainted with the spirit of the place, sat lunching alone. Stevenson, desiring to welcome him and make him feel at home, went over and opened talk in his most gracious manner. His advance was received with cold rebuff and the implied intimation that the stranger desired no company but his own. Stevenson came away furious, and presently relieved his wrath with the lampoon which is included in his published works and begins (the offender being made to speak in the first person):

I am a kind of farthing dip
Unfriendly to the nose and eyes.

But to turn from such social memories, which will be shared by a dwindling band of survivors from the middle and late seventies, to those private to myself: — it was in the early summer of 1874, soon after the appearance of his second published paper, *Ordered South*, that he spent a fortnight with me in my quarters on Hampstead Hill. One morning, while I was attending to my own affairs, I was aware of Stevenson craning intently out of a side window and watching something. Presently he turned with a radiant countenance and the thrill of happiness in his voice to bid me come and watch too. A group of girl children were playing with the skipping-rope a few yards down the lane. "Was there ever such heavenly sport? Had I ever seen anything so beautiful? Kids and a skipping-rope — most of all that blessed youngest kid with the broken nose who didn't know how to skip — nothing in the whole wide world had ever made him half so happy in his life before." Scarce any one else would have given a second look or thought to the little scene; but while it lasted it held him thus entranced in the eagerness of observation, and exclaiming through all the gamut of superlatives. From such superlatives, corresponding to the ardour and intensity of his being, his talk at all times derived much of its colour. During ill-health, had he a day or an hour of respite, he would gleefully proclaim himself a balmy being and a bird of Paradise. Did anything in life or literature please him, it was for the moment inimitably and incomparably the most splendid and wonderful thing in the whole world, and he must absolutely have you think so too — unless, indeed, you chose to direct his sense of humour against his own exaggerations, in which case he would generally receive your criticism with ready assenting laughter. But not quite always, if the current of feeling was too strong. My wife reminds me of an incident in point, from the youthful time when he used to make her the chief confidante of his troubles and touchstone of his tastes. One day he came to her with an early, I think the

Travels with a Donkey frontispiece by Walter Crane

earliest, volume of poems by Mr Robert Bridges, the present poet-laureate, in his hand; declared here was the most wonderful new genius, and enthusiastically read out to her some of the contents in evidence; till becoming aware that they were being coolly received, he leapt up crying, "My God! I believe you don't like them," and flung the book across the room and himself out of the house in a paroxysm of disappointment — to return a few hours later and beg pardon humbly for his misbehaviour. But for some time afterwards, whenever he desired her judgment on work of his own or others, he would begin by bargaining: "You won't *Bridges* me this time, will you?" Sometimes, indeed, when he meant something stronger even than usual, he would himself disarm the critic, and at the same time heighten his effect, by employing a figure not of exaggeration but of humorous diminution, and would cover the intensity of his feeling by expressing it in some perfectly colourless, flat hack phrase. You would propose something you knew he was red-hot to do, and he would reply, his eyes flashing with anticipation, "Well, yes. He could bring himself to do that without a pang": or he would describe the horrors of a visit to the dentist or of a formal tea-party (to one or two of which he was about this time lured), by admitting that it hadn't been quite all his fancy painted it; which you knew meant a degree of tribulation beyond superlatives.

Nothing proved to my mind Stevenson's true vocation to literature, or encouraged me more to push him under the notice of editors, than the way in which he exercised from the first a firm artistic control over his own temperament, suppressing his tendency to exaggerations and superlatives and practising a deliberate moderation of statement and lenity of style. This was very apparent when the little scene outside our lodging-house window, mingling in memory with the pleasure he had lately experienced at Mentone in waatching the staggering evolutions of his Russian baby friend Nelitchka, suggested to him the essay, "Notes on the Movements of Young Children," which was printed in the *Portfolio* (then edited by Philip Gilbert Hamerton) for the following August. The little paper, which he did not think worth reprinting in his life-time but is to be found in the posthumous editions, seemed to me an extraordinarily promising effort at analytic description half-humorous, half-tender — and promising above all in as far as it proved how well, while finding brilliantly effective expression for the subtlety of vital observation which was one part of his birthright, he could hold in check the tendency to emotional stress and vehemence which was another. This was in itself a kind of distinction in an age when so many of our prose-writers, and those the most attractive and impressive to youth, as Carlyle, Macaulay, Ruskin, Dickens, were men who, for all their genius, lacked or did not seek the special virtues of restraint and lenity of style, but were given, each after his manner, to strenuous emphasis, to splendid over-colouring and over-heightening: dealers in the purple patch and the insistent phrase, the vehement and contentious assertion.

The next scene which comes up with a special vividness in my memory dates, I think, from a year or two later. Of very young children his love was not, as I have said, always at once returned by them; but over growing boys of whatever class or breeding his spell was apt to be instantaneous. City arabs felt it just as much as any others. One day, as he and I had just come out from a meditative stroll through St. Paul's Cathedral, we found outselves near a little ragged troop of such. With one of his characteristic smiles, full of love and mischief, he immediately, at a first glance, seemed to establish a roguish understanding with them. They grinned back and closed about him and clung to him as we walked, fastening eager looks on his, held and drawn by they knew not what expectation: no, not by the hope of coppers, but by something more human — more divine, if you like to put it so — that had beamed upon their poor little souls from his looks. The small crowd of them kept growing and still surrounding us. As it was impossible for him at that place and moment practically to provide adventure or entertainment for them, it became a little difficult to know what to do. At last I solved the situation tamely, by calling a hansom cab and carrying my friend off in it. More by token, that same hansom horse, I remember, presently got the bit between his teeth and bolted for some half a mile along the Thames Embankment; and while I sat with stiffened knees and nerves on the stretch, expecting a smash, I could see that Stevenson actually enjoyed it. Few of us, chiefly because the build of the vehicle kept the driver's hands and hold upon the reins out of sight, were ever truly happy in a bolting hansom; but Stevenson was so made that any kind of danger was a positive physical exhilaration to him.

Of the visits which he paid to me at Cambridge in these years, the retrospect had again generalized itself for the most part into vagueness, a mere abstract sense of forgotton talk ranging from the most red-blooded human to the airiest elfin. One impression which was always strong upon him there, and I think is recorded somewhere in his letters, is the profound difference between these English universities, with their beauty and dignity of aspect, their venerable college buildings and fair avenues and gardens, and anything which exists in Scotland, where residential colleges form no part of university life. Such surroundings used to affect him with a sense almost of unreality, as something romantically pleasurable but hardly credible; and this sense came most strongly upon him when I left him alone for some days in occupation of my rooms, with gyps and porters at his beck, while I went off on business elsewhere. Of personal relations which he formed there the only one I specially remember was with that interesting character, the late A.G. Dew-Smith. Dew-Smith, or Dew, as his friends called him for short, was a man of fine tastes and of means to gratify them. As a resident master of arts he helped the natural science departments by starting and superintending a workshop for manufacturing instruments of research of the most perfect make and finish; and he was one of the most skilful of photographers, alike in the scientific and artistic uses of the craft — a certain large-scale carbon print he took of Stevenson to my mind comes nearer to the original in richness of character and expression than any other portrait. He was a collector of rare prints and other treasures, including precious stones, of which in their uncut state he would sometimes pull a handful out of his pocket to show us. He was tall, with finely cut features, black silky hair and neatly pointed beard, and withal a peculiarly soft and silken, deliberate manner of speech. Considerable were our surprise and amusement when some dozen years later we found his outward looks and bearing, and particularly his characteristic turns of speech, with something of dangerous power which his presence suggested as lying behind so much polished blandness, evoked and idealized by Stevenson in his creation of the personage of Attwater in that grimmest of island stories, *The Ebb Tide*. In telling anything of special interest that had happened to himself, Dew-Smith had a trick of avoiding the first person singular, and instead of saying "I did" or "I felt" so and so would say abstractly in the third, "one did" or "one felt." This scrupulous manner

of non-egotism, I remember, came with specially odd effect when one day he was telling us how an official at a railway station had been offensively rude to him. "What did you do?" he was asked, and replied in a deprecating voice, "Well, you know, one had to put him through the door-panels." It is this aspect of Dew-Smith's character which no doubt suggested, although it did not really much resemble, the ruthless task-master, the man of stern Calvinistic doctrine and iron fatalism, who is the other half of Stevenson's Attwater.

Stevenson has interpreted the aspects and the thrill of out-door nature as magically as anyone in written words, but was not prone to talk about them. "No human being ever spoke of scenery for above two minutes at a time," he declares in his essay on *Talk and Talkers*; and I cannot remember that he used ever to say much about the forest of Fontainebleau or the other scenes in France which he loved so well and frequented so much in these years, or even about those excursions which he was busy turning to such happy literary account in *An Inland Voyage* and *Travels with a Donkey*. Literature and human life were ever his main themes; including sometimes, but of course with his closest intimates only, the problems of his own life. By and by such intimates became aware that these problems had taken on a new and what might easily have turned into a tragical complexity. He had been for some time in the habit of frequenting the artist haunts of the Fontainebleau forest in the company of his cousin Bob Stevenson, for the sake of health and ease of mind and of the open-air life and congenial irresponsible company he found there. In those haunts it presently became apparent he had met his fate. To escape from hopeless conjugal troubles, a Mrs Osbourne[2] from California, we learnt, had come and for the time being settled there with her daughter and young son. She was some dozen years older than Stevenson, but fate had destined them for each other, and their momentary mutual attraction soon settled — for each other was as far as possible from being a light-o'-love — into the unbreakable bond of a life-time. After a while the lady had to return to California, and there sought and

---

[2] Colvin in fact wrote 'Strong', clearly a slip. Stevenson's future wife's name was Fanny Van de Grift Osbourne. 'Strong' was Fanny's daughter's married name.

was able to obtain freedom by divorce. Stevenson had promptly followed her, saying nothing of his intention to his parents, who he knew would disapprove it, and trusting wholly to the meagre resources he was in those days able to command by his pen. Then followed for those of us who loved him and were in the secret a period of sore anxiety. There reached us from time to time scanty news of his discomforts undergone in the emigrant ship and train, and of his dangerous and complicated illnesses afterwards, and evidences withal of his indomitable will and courage in the shape of new tales and essays composed for his livelihood in circumstances under which any less resolute spirit must have sunk. Reconciled with his parents after a while by the fact of his marriage, he brought his wife home to them in the late summer of 1880. She made an immediate conquest of them, especially of that character so richly compounded between the stubborn and the tender, the humorous and the grim, his father. Thenceforth there was always at Louis's side a wife for his friends to hold only second in affection to himself. A separate biography of her by her sister has lately appeared, giving, along with many interested details of her early life, a picture of her on the whole softer and less striking than that which I personally retain. Strength and staunchness were, as I saw her, her ruling qualities; strength and staunchness not indeed masculine in their kind, but truly womanly. Against those of his friends who might forget or ignore the precautions which his health demanded she could be a dragon indeed; but the more considerate among them she made warmly her own and was ever ready to welcome. Deep and rich capacities were in her, alike for tragedy and humour; all her moods, thoughts, and instincts were vividly genuine and her own, and her daily talk, like her letters, was admirable both for play of character and feeling and for choice and colour of words. On those who knew the pair first after their marriage her personality impressed itself almost as vividly as his; and in my own mind his image lives scarce more indelibly than that of the small, dark-complexioned, eager, devoted woman his mate. In spite of her squareish build she was supple and elastic in all her movements; her hands and feet were small and beautifully modelled, though not meant for, or used to, idleness; the head, under its crop of close-waving thick black hair, was of a build

and character that somehow suggested Napoleon, by firm setting of the jaw and the beautifully precise and delicate modelling of the nose and lips: the eyes were full of sex and mystery as they changed from fire or fun to gloom or tenderness; and it was from between a fine pearly set of small teeth that there came the clear metallic accents of her intensely human and often quaintly individual speech.

The journey to California, with its risks and hardships, had had results as damaging to Stevenson's health as they were needful and fruitful for his happiness. After his return in the late summer of 1880 it was under much more positively invalid conditions than before that his friends found themselves obliged to seek his company. My chief special recollections of him during the next few years date almost entirely from places where he had gone in hopes of recovery or respite from his complicated and crippling troubles of nerve, artery and lung. Just as little as the restrictions of the sick-room, galling to him above all men, had power to hinder his industry and success as a writer, so little did they impair his charm as a talker when he was allowed to talk at all. Occasionally, and oftener as time went on, haemorrhages from the lung, or the immediate threat of them, enforced upon him periods of absolute silence, during which he could only communicate on paper with those about him, writing with blotting-pad against his knees as he lay in his red flannel dressing-gown propped against pillows in his bed. But in the intervals of respite his friends had the happiness of finding life and letters and art, experience and the possibilities of experience, once more irradiated for them as vividly as before, or even more vividly yet, in the glow and magic of his conversation.

For the first two years after his return Stevenson spent the winters (1880-81, 1881-2) at the Swiss mountain station of Davos, which had just begun to come into repute as a place of cure, and the summers at one resort or another in the bracing climate of the Scottish Highlands. The Davos of 1880, approached by a laborious seven hours' sledge-ride and vastly different from the luxurious and expanded Davos of to-day, consisted of the old Swiss village of Davos-Platz, clustered round its high-spired church, with one central group of German hotels in or close adjoining the village, and another smaller but more scattered group of English hotels at a little distance beside the open road in the direction of the minor village of Davos-Dorf. The Stevenson quarters for this first winter were at the Hotel Belvedere, then a mere miniature nucleus of its latter-day self. I shall never forget his first reception of me there. It was about Christmas, 1880; I arrived late; and the moment dinner was over he had me out and up a short hill at the back of the hotel. There had only lately fallen enough snow to allow the sport of tobogganing to be started: there was a steep zigzag run down from a hut on the hill to near the hotel: he got me into the toboggan by moonlight, we started down the run, capsized at a corner, rolled over and over with our mouths and pockets full of snow, and walked home in tearing spirits. Nothing could have been more like him, and nothing (of course) much worse for him. My impression of the next few weeks at Davos is one of high tension of the soul and body in that tingling mountain air, under the iron moonlit frosts or the mid-day dazzle of the snowfields; of the haunting sense of tragedy (of one tragedy in especial which touched us both to the heart) among that company, for the most part doomed or stricken, with faces tanned by sun and frost into masks belying their real plight: of endless bouts of eager, ever courteous give-and-take over the dark Valtellina wine between Stevenson and John Addington Symonds, in whom he had found a talker almost as charming as himself, exceeding him by far in range and accuracy of knowledge and culture, as was to be expected in the author of the *History of the Renaissance in Italy*, but nothing like his match, I thought, in essential sanity of human judgment or in the power of illumination by unforeseeable caprices of humour and fantasy. The reader can if he pleases turn to Stevenson's own impression of these conversations, whether as generalized afterward in the essay *Talk and Talkers*, where Symonds figures as Opalstein, or as set down in a letter at the time:— "I like Symonds very well, though he is much, I think, of an invalid in mind and character. But his mind is interesting, with many beautiful corners, and his consumptive smile very winning to see. We have had some good talks; one went over Zola, Balzac, Flaubert, Whitman, Christ, Handel, Milton, Sir Thomas Browne; do you see the *liaison*? — in another, I, the Bohnist, the un-Grecian, was

the means of his conversion in the matter of the Ajax." It is interesting to compare with these words Symond's own retrospect on the same days and talks written six years after Stevenson's death: "I have never lived in Davos a better time than I lived then; it has been so full of innocent jollity and beautiful Bohemianism, so sweetened by the strong clear spirit of that unique sprite whom all the world claims for its own now — R.L. Stevenson . . . So gracious and so pure a light has never fallen upon my path as fell from his fantastic and yet intensely human genius — the beautiful companionship of the Shelley-like man, the eager, gifted wife, and the boy for whom they both thought in all their ways and hours."

Neither from the first of the two Highland summers nor the second Alpine winter do I retain any impressions as strong and definite as those I have last set down, though I was with him for a part of both, and though the August and September weeks of 1881 at Braemar were marked by the excitement of the first conception and discussion of the tale of *The Sea-Cook*, which afterward developed into *Treasure Island*. They were remarkable also for the disgust of the patient at being condemned to wear a specially contrived and hideous kind of pig's-snout respirator for the inhalation of pine-oil, as related in a well known rhyming letter of the time to Henley. But from the second Highland summer dates another vivid recollection. While his wife remained with his parents at Edinburgh, I spent two or three weeks of radiant weather alone with him in the old hotel at Kingussie in Inverness-shire. He had little strength either for work or exercise but managed to draft the tale *The Treasure of Franchard*, and rejoiced in lying out for hours at a time half stripped in the sun, nearly according to that manner of sun-bath since so much prescribed by physicians in Germany. The burn or mountain streamlet at the back of Kingussie village is for about a mile of its course after it leaves the moor one of the most varied and beautiful in Scotland, racing with a hundred little falls and lynns beside the margin of an enchanting fir-belted, green and dingled oval glade. The glade, alas, has long ago been invaded and annexed by golfers, enemies to peace; and even the approaches to the burn from the village have, I understand, been ruined by the erection of a great modern distillery. But in the year 1882 we had those haunts to ourselves. Stevenson used to spend hours exploring the recesses of the burn's course, musing, sometimes with and sometimes without speech, on its endless chances and caprices of eddy and ripple and back-set, its branchings and reunitings, alternations of race and pool, bustle and pause, and on the images of human life, free-will, and destiny presented by the careers of the sticks and leaves he found or launched upon its course. One result of these musings occurs in a dramatic scene familiar to all who have read his fragment, *The Great North Road*. Of other talk what I remember best is the entertainment with which he read for the first time Leigh Hunt's milk-and-water dilution of Dante in his poem *Francesca da Rimini* (or *Nimini-pimini* as Byron re-christened it), and of the laughing parodies which bubbled over from him on those passages of tea-party sentiment and cockney bathos that disfigure it. Some kind of play, too, I remember which he insisted on starting and keeping up, and wherein he invested his companion (that was me) with the imaginary character of a roystering blade in a white greatcoat and knobstick making scandal in the Highland village, and himself with that of a sedate and friendly burgess hard put to it to save me from the hands of the police.

The following winter took the Stevensons to the Provençal coast, but to haunts there at some distance from those he had known ten years ago. After some unsuccessful attempts to settle near Marseilles (Stevenson always loved the colour and character of that mighty Mediterranean and cosmopolitan trading-port), they were established by March 1884, in the Châlet la Solitude on the hill behind Hyères; and on that charming site he enjoyed the best months of health and happiness he ever knew, at least on the European continent. His various expressions in prose and verse of pleasure in his life there are well-known. For instance, the following from a letter to Mr Gosse:— "This pot, our garden and our view, are sub-celestial. I sing daily with my Bunyan, that great bard,

I dwell already the next door to Heaven!

If you could see my roses, and my aloes, and my fig-marigolds, and my olives, and my view over a plain, and my view of certain mountains as graceful as Apollo, as severe as Zeus, you would not think the phrase exaggerated." One or two sets of verses dallying with the notion that here might be his permanent home and anchorage have only lately been published. I give another set written in a somewhat homelier strain, which I think has not yet found its way into print:

My wife and I, in our romantic cot,
The world forgetting, by the world forgot,
High as the gods upon Olympus dwell,
Pleased with the things we have, and pleased as well
To wait in hope for those which we have not.

She burns in ardour for a horse to trot;
I pledge my votive powers upon a yacht;
Which shall be first remembered, who can tell —
*   My wife or I?*

Harvests of flowers o'er all our garden-plot
She dreams; and I to enrich a darker spot,
My umprovided cellar; both to swell
Our narrow cottage huge as a hotel,
That portly friends may come and share our lot —
*   My wife and I.*

The first friend to come was one not physically corresponding to the adjective, namely myself. It was the moment when the Southern spring was in its first flush and freshness, and the days and evenings sped gloriously. Everything, down to the *dèche* or money pinch to which recent expenses had reduced him, or the misdeeds of the black Skye-terrier Woggs, the most engaging, petted, ill-conducted and cajoling little thorough-bred rascal of his race, was turned by Stevenson into a matter of abounding delight or diversion. No schemes of work could for the time being seem too many or too arduous. A flow of verse, more continuous and varied than ever before, had set in from him. Besides many occasional pieces expressing intimate moods of the moment with little care or finish, and never intended for any eye but his own, those of the special *Child's Garden* series were nearly completed; and they and their dedication, as in duty bound, to his old nurse Alison Cunningham had to be canvassed between us. So had a much more arduous matter, the scheme and style of *Prince Otto*, its general idea having gradually, under much discussion, been evolved from an earlier one where the problems and characters would have been similar but the setting and date Oriental and remote. So had a scheme to be put in hand next after that, namely, a new tale for boys; this time a historical tale, which duly took shape as *The Black Arrow*, to be slighted later on, quite unjustly as I have always thought, by its author and his family as "tushery."

One day, looking from one of the hill terraces from near his house at the group of islets (the isles of Hyères) in the offing, we had let our talk wander to famous and more distant archipelagoes of the same inland sea. I spoke of the likeness in unlikeness which strikes the traveller between the noble outlines and colours of the Ionian group, as they rise facing the coasts of Acarnania, Elis, and Epirus, and those of the group of the Inner Hebrides over against the shores of Ross and Argyleshire. We ran over the blunt monosyllabic names of some of the Hebridean group — Coll, Mull, Eigg, Rum, Muck, and Skye — and contrasted them with the euphonious Greek sounds, Leucadia, Cephalonia, Ithaca, Zante or Zacynthos ("Jam medio apparet fluctu nemorosa Zacynthos" had for some unaccountable reason been Stevenson's favourite line of Virgil from boyhood, and he goes out of his way to make occasion for one of his characters to quote it in almost the latest of his sea-tales, *The Ebb Tide*). And we speculated on a book written that should try to strike the several notes of these two island regions, of their scenery, inhabitants, and traditions, of Greek and Gaelic lay and legend, and the elements of Homeric and Ossianic poetry. I think the idea was no bad one, and that perhaps such a book has still to be, and will some day be, written. But Stevenson, with his lack of Greek and of the Greek scholar's special enthusiasm, and the unlikelihood of his being able to work much in libraries, would perhaps hardly have been the man to attempt it. Nevertheless, having frequented the Hebrides group and drunk in its romance from youth in the lighthouse yacht, and again on a special excursion with Sir Walter Simpson in 1874, he was much attracted by the scheme. And when some eight months later, by what I believe was a pure coincidence, he received a proposal from a firm of publishers that he should take a cruise in the Greek archipelago with a view to a volume that should tell of his experiences in a manner something like that of his former small volumes of travel in France, our talk of the spring, recurring to him, made him take warmly to the notion. He wrote to me at once on the question of introductions, and went to Nice, partly to

Fanny Osbourne

make inquiries about Mediterranean steam-packets and partly to ask medical advice. The latter confirmed, I believe, what was the judgment of his wife that the risks of the trip would be too great; and the idea was dropped.

In my next glimpse of him there were elements of comedy. I had gone for a few weeks' travel in Southern Italy, and meaning to return by sea and across France from Naples, with a very short time to spare before I was due back in London, had asked the Stevensons if they would come and meet me for a day or so at Marseilles. They came, and it was a happy meeting. But I discovered that I had miscalculated travelling expenses and had not enough cash in hand to finish my homeward journey. He found himself in the proud position of being able to help me, but only at the cost of leaving his own pockets empty. He had to remain in Marseilles until I could reimburse him from Paris, and amused himself with some stanzas in honour of the place and the occasion:

> Long time I lay in little ease
> Where, paced by the Turanian,
> Marseilles, the many-masted, sees
> The blue Mediterranean.
>
> Now songful in the hour of sport,
> Now riotous for wages,
> She camps around her ancient port,
> An ancient of the ages.
>
> Algerian airs through all the place
> Unconquerably sally;
> Incomparable women pace
> The shadows of the alley.
>
> And high o'er dock and graving-yard
> And where the sky is paler,
> The Golden Virgin of the Guard
> Shines, beckoning the sailor.
>
> She hears the city roar on high,
> Thief, prostitute, and banker;
> She sees the masted vesels lie
> Immovably at anchor.
>
> She sees the snowy islets dot
> The sea's immortal azure,
> And If, that castellated spot,
> Tower, turret and embrazure.
>
> Here Dantès pined; and here to-day
> Behold me his successor:
> For here imprisoned long I lay
> In pledge for a professor!*

*In the recent volume, New Poems, this little piece has unluckily been published with the misprints "placed" for "paced" in the first stanza, "as" for "an" in the second, and "dark" for "dock" in the fourth; the last stanza, which gives the whole its only point and raison d'être, being left out. The allusions concerning Dantès and the Chateau d'If point, of course, to the Monte Cristo of the elder Dumas.

Seven or eight months later a violent and all but fatal return of illness dashed the high hopes which had been raised by the happy Provençal spring and summer. An epidemic of cholera following made him leave the Mediterranean shore for good and sent him home to England. He arrived to all appearance and according to almost all medical prognostics a confirmed and even hopeless invalid. His home for the next three years was at Bournemouth. He was subject to frequent haemorrhages from the lung, any of which might have proved fatal and which had to be treated with styptic remedies of the strongest and most nerveshaking kind. Much of his life was spent on the sofa, much in that kind of compulsory silence which up till now had at worst been only occasional. Now and again a few weeks of respite enabled him to make cautious excursions, once as far as Paris, once to Matlock, once or more on my invitation to Cambridge, but oftenest to London. Here his resort was not to hotels, but as an ever-welcome guest to the official house I had lately come to inhabit within the gates of the British Museum. His industry, maintained against harder conditions than ever, showed itself all the more indomitable and at last had its reward. The success of Treasure Island published before he left Hyères, was by the time he settled at Bournemouth beginning to make his name a popular one. Two and a half years later Jekyll and Hyde raised it suddenly into resounding fame, and was immediately followed by Kidnapped which was by common consent acclaimed as the best Scotch tale since the Waverleys. For part of the Bournemouth time he was also much engaged in joint work with Henley on the plays Admiral Guinea, Beau Austin, and Macaire: and upon this, the lustiest and not always the most considerate of guests and collaborators, Mrs Stevenson found herself compelled in the interest of her husband's health to lay restrictions which were resented, and sowed the first seeds, I think, of that estrangement at heart of Henley from his friend so lamentably proclaimed by him in public after Stevenson's death.

Ill as he was in these years, Stevenson was able to bind to himself in close friendship not a few new-comers, including two eminent Americans, Henry James and the painter J.S. Sargent. I went down myself from time to time, and enjoyed his company not less, only with more of anxiety and misgiving, than of old. Sargent's little picture showing him indescribably lean in his velvet jacket as he paces to and fro twirling his moustache with one hand and holding his cigarette in the other as he talks — St. Gaudens's bronze relief of him propped on pillows on the sofa (the latter a work done two or three years later in America) — these tally pretty closely in their different ways with the images I carry in my mind of his customary looks and attitudes in those Bournemouth days. Always except once I found him as cheerful as ever, and as vivid a focus of cheerfulness. The sole exception remains deeply printed on my memory. I had followed him from the house into the garden; he was leaning with his back to me looking out from the garden gate; as he heard me approach, he turned round upon me a face such as I never saw on him save that once — a face of utter despondency, nay tragedy, upon which seemed stamped for one concentrated moment the expression of all he had ever had, or might yet have, in life to suffer or to renounce. Such a countenance was not to be accosted, and I left him. During his visits to my house at the British Museum — "the many-pillared and the well-beloved," as he calls it in the well-known set of verses, as though the keepers' houses stood within the great front colonnade of the museum, which they do not, but project in advance of it on either flank — during such visits he never showed anything but the old charm and high courage and patience. He was able to enjoy something of the company of famous seniors who came seeking his acquaintance, as Browning, Lowell, Burne-Jones. With such visitors I usually left him alone, and have at any rate no detailed notes or memories of conversations held by him with them in my presence. What I remember most vividly was how one day I came in from my work and found the servants, who were devoted to him, waiting for me in the hall with scared faces. He had had a worse haemorrhage than usual, and lay propped on his pillows in his red dressing-grown with pencil in hand and foolscap paper against his knees. He greeted me with finger on lip and a smile half humorous half ruefully deprecating, as though in apology for being so troublesome a guest; handing me at the same time a sheet on which he had written the words from Falstaff, "'Tis my vocation, Hal." Then, with a changed look of expectant curiosity and adventure, he wrote, "Do you think it will *faucher* me this time?" (French *faucher*, to mow down, to kill, make an end of.) I forget how

the conversation, spoken on my side, written on his, went on. With his intimates and those of his household he held many such, and it would have been interesting to keep the sheets on which his side of the talk, often illustrated with comic sketches, was set down. So would it have been interesting to keep another record of the same illness, namely the little lumps or pats of modellers' wax which he asked me to get for him and with which, when he could not talk, read or write, he amused himself moulding tiny scenes with figures and landscapes in relief. These were technically childish, of course, but had always, like the woodcuts done to amuse his stepson at Davos, a touch of lively expressiveness and character. Some dozens of them, I remember, he finished, but no vestige of them remains. They were put into a drawer, dried, cracked, and were thrown away.

My next vision of him is the last, and shows him as he stood with his family looking down upon me over the rail of the outward-bound steamship *Ludgate Hill* while I waved a parting hand to him from a boat in the Thames by Tilbury Dock. From our first meeting in Suffolk until his return with his wife from California in 1880 had been one spell of seven years. From that return until his fresh departure in 1887 had been another. Now followed the winter spent at Saranac Lake in the Adirondack mountains; the two years and odd months of cruising among the various archipelagoes of the Pacific — the Marquesas, the Paumotus, the Society Islands, the Sandwich group, Samoa, the Gilberts again, the Marshalls. The lure of the South Seas and the renewed capacity for out-door life and adventure he found in himself during these voyagings had gradually forced upon both Stevenson and his wife the conclusion that there was but one thing for him to do, and that was to settle somewhere in the Pacific for good. He had written as much to his friends in England, telling them at the same time of the property he had bought in Samoa and on which he proposed to build himself a home. Several earlier letters which would have prepared us for this news had miscarried, so that when the announcement came it was a rude shock to those who loved him and were looking forward eagerly to his return. At Sydney, in August, 1890, he received our replies. Mine was of a tenor which cut the warm hearts of both the pair to the quick, although not

'Kidnapped'

serving to deflect their purpose. In spite of the fine work he had done during his voyages, I persuaded myself that from living permanently in that outlandish world and far from cultivated society both he and his writing must deteriorate, and wrote warning him as much in plain terms. Translating unconsciously my own need and desire for his company into a persuasion that mine was needed, as of old, for criticism and suggestion to him in his work, and that he no longer valued it, I wrote reproachfully, pleading against and prophesying evil from his purpose. He and his wife both set themselves then and there to justify their decision in letters of which, reverting to them now after thirty years, I find the terms infinitely touching and too sacred almost to quote.

Referring to one of his recent cruises, Stevenson says:

> We had a very delightful voyage for some part; it would have been delightful to the end had my health held out. That it did not, I attribute to savage hard work in a wild cabin heated like the Babylonian furnace, four plies of blotting-paper under my wet hand and the drops trailing from my brow. For God's sake don't start in to blame Fanny: often enough she besought me not to go on: but I did my work while I was a bedridden worm in England, and please God I shall do my work until I burst. I do not know any other virtue that I possess; and indeed there are few others I prize alongside of it. Only, one other I have: I love my friends, and I don't like to hear the most beloved of all casting doubt on that affection. Did you not get the verses I sent you from Apemama? I guess they were not A1 verses, but they expressed something you surely could not doubt.* But perhaps all my letters have miscarried? A sorrow on correspondence! If this miscarry too? See here: if by any chance this should come to your hand, understand once and for all that since my dear wild noble father died no head on earth is more precious to my thoughts than yours. . . But all this talk is useless. Know this, I love you, and since I am speaking plainly for once, I bind it upon you as sacred duty, should you be dangerously ill, I must be summoned. I will never forgive you if I am not. So long as there is no danger, I do well, do I not? — to consider conditions necessary to my work and health. I have a charge of souls; I keep many eating and drinking; my continued life has a value of its own; and I cannot but feel it. But I have to see you again. That is sure. And — how strangely we are made! — I see no harm in my dying like a burst pig upon some outlandish island, but if you died, without due notice and a chance for me to see you, I should count it a disloyalty.

> *These are the verses "To S.C." afterwards printed as No. XXXVI in the volume *Songs of Travel*. In point of fact the package containing them had for the time being failed to reach me.

Here Stevenson's hand failed and his wife takes up the letter, and in many urgent, not less affectionate phrases continues to enforce his plea:

> DEAR CUSTODIAN,—
>
> I hardly dare use that word with the knowledge in my heart that we intend to remove our bodily selves from out your custody, but as you know it will be our vile bodies only; spiritually we are yours and always will be. Neither time nor space can change us in that. You told me when we left England if we found a place where Louis was really well to stay there. It really seems that anywhere in the South Seas will do. Ever since we have been here we have been on the outlook for a spot that combines the most advantages. In some way I preferred the Marquesas, the climate being perfect and the natives people that I admired and loved. The only suitable place on the Sandwich islands is at the foot of a volcano where we should have to live upon black lava and trust to rain for water. Besides I could not bear the white population. All things considered, Samoa took our fancy the most; there are three opportunities each month to communicate with England by telegraph from Auckland, Auckland being from seven to eight days' steam distance from us. You could hardly believe your own eyes if you could see Louis in his present state of almost rude health, no cough, no haemorrhage, no night sweats. He rides and walks as much as he likes without any fatigue, and in fact lives the life of a man who is well. I tremble when I think of a return to England.

He never returned to England, and a third spell of seven years in his life had just been completed when on one gloomy, gusty, sodden December day in 1894, I came down from lunching with Sir Harry Johnston, the African traveller and administrator, in the upper floor of a Government office in Westminster, and saw newspaper posters flapping dankly in the street corners, with the words "Death of R.L. Stevenson" printed large upon them. The Pacific voyages and the island life had, or seemed to have, effectually healed his troubles of nerve, throat, and lung; but the old arterial weakness remained, and after so many years of unsparing mental toil the bursting of a blood-vessel in his brain had laid him low at the critical moment of his fully ripening power.

During that third and last period the day-dreams of the Mentone days had after all and in spite of all and against all likelihood been realized for him. Fame as a writer even beyond his aspirations had come to be his. Of voyagings in far-off oceans, of happy out-door activities and busy beneficent responsibilities in romantic circumstances and outlandish scenes, he had had his fill. Withal his love of his old friends had amid his new experiences and successes never weakened. Of this no one had ampler or more solid proofs than I. That amidst all his other absorbing interests, and in spite of his ever-growing passion and assiduity in literary work, he should never once have failed in sending off to me his regular full budget of a monthly letter, either written with his own hand or dictated to his step-daughter, would have been proof enough in itself of such steadfastness. On the side of his friends at home, speaking at least for myself, I fear that our joy in the news of his returning strength and activity had been tempered by something of latent jealousy that so much good could befall him without help of ours and at a distance of half the world away from us. I know that I was inclined to be hypercritical about the quality and value of some of the work sent home from the Pacific. I thought the series of papers afterwards arranged into the volume *In the South Seas* overloaded with information and the results of study, and disappointingly lacking in the thrill and romance one expected of him in relating experiences which had realized the dream of his youth. (I ought to mention that a far better qualified judge, Mr Joseph Conrad, differs from me in this, and even prefers *In the South Seas* to *Treasure Island*, principally for the sake of what he regards as a very masterpiece of native portraiture in the character of Tembinok, King of Apemama.)

Again, I thought it a pity that Stevenson should spend so much toil in setting out, in the volume *A Footnote to History*, the details of certain complicated, very remote and petty recent affairs in which none except perhaps a few international diplomatists could well be expected to take interest. Of his work in fiction dealing with the islands, I thought most of *The Wrecker* below his mark, and *The Ebb Tide*, at least the first half of it, a comparatively dull and rather brutal piece of realism. True, there were collaboration pieces; and of island stories there was *The Beach of Falesà*, and of Scottish tales *Catriona*, which were all his own and of which the quality should have fully re-assured one (the master-fragment *Weir of Hermiston* was of course unknown to us till after his death). But thinking as I did, I said so in my letters with the old frankness, causing him for once a shade of displeasure: for he wrote to me that I was being a little too Cockney with him, and to a common friend that I was getting to be something of an auld wife with my criticisms. Well, well, perhaps I was, perhaps not. But at any rate I have proof in full measure that his affection for and memory of me survived and underwent no change. One such proof, scarce less surprising than endearing, came to me but the other day,

long after his death, in the shape of a bulky packet sent to me by his representatives in America. On opening the packet I found that it contained almost the whole mass of my letters written to him from the beginning of our friendship to the end. Considering the vagrant habits of his youth, his long dislike of and detachment from all the ordinary *impedimenta* of life, his frequent changes of abode even after marriage and success had made of him a comparatively settled and propertied man — considering these things, that he should have cumbered himself by the preservation of so bulky a correspondence was a thing to me naturally undreamed of and when discovered infinitely touching. As concerns my regard and regret for him, — there has been hardly a day in the thirty and odd years since he left us on which I, like others who loved him, have not missed him. His cousin Bob Stevenson, in some gifts and brilliancies almost his match, used to vow that the chief interest of anything which happened was to hear what Louis would say about it. World-events in war and politics and mankind's material experiments and physical conquests in the last few years have been too tremendous in themselves for so much to be said of any man without absurdity. But want him and long for him one does, to hear him talk both of them and of a thousand lesser things: most of all perhaps of those writers who have stepped into fame since his time. If we could have him back among us, as one sometimes has him in day-dreams, how we, his old friends and comrades in letters — but alas! with what gaps among us, Henry James gone, Andrew Lang gone, and so many others — how would we make haste to gather about him: and when we had had our turn, how eagerly would he look round for the younger fellow-craftsmen, Sir James Barrie, Mr Kipling — not now indeed so young — whose promise he had recognized and with whom in his last years he had exchanged greetings across the ocean. Of those who had not begun to publish before he died the man I imagine him calling for first of all is the above-mentioned Mr Conrad. Some time about 1880-90 these two seafarers, the Polish gentleman turned British merchant-skipper and the ocean-loving author cruising far and wide in search of health, might quite well have met in life, only that the archipelago of Mr Conrad's chief experiences was the Malay, that of Stevenson's the Polynesian. Could my dream be fulfilled, how they would

SKERRYVORE

ere all is sunny and when the truant gull
Skims the green level of the lawn, his wing
Dispetals roses; here the house is framed
Of kneaded brick and the plumed mountain pine
Such clay as artists fashion and such wood
As the tree climbing urchin breaks

delight in meeting now. What endless ocean and island yarns the two would exchange; how happily they would debate the methods and achievements of their common art; and how difficult it would be to part them! As I let myself imagine such meeting, I know not which of the two presences is the more real and near to me, yours, my good friend Conrad, whom I hope and mean to greet in the flesh to-morrow or the next day or the next, or that of Stevenson, since my last sight of whom, as he waved good-bye to me from the deck of the "Ludgate Hill." I know as a fact of arithmetic, but can in no other sense realize, that there has passed a spell of no less than four-and thirty years or the life-time of a whole generation.

Robert Louis Stevenson
EDMUND GOSSE

PERSONAL MEMORIES

In setting down my recollections of Louis Stevenson, I desire to confine the record to what I have myself known and seen. His writings will be mentioned only in so far as I heard them planned and discussed. Of his career and character I shall not attempt to give a complete outline; all I purpose to do is to preent those sides of them which came under my personal notice. The larger portrait it will be his privilege to prepare who was the closest and most responsible of all Stevenson's friends; and it is only while we wait for Mr Sydney Colvin's biography that these imperfect sketches can retain their value. The most that can be hoped for them is that they may secure a niche in his gallery. And now, pen in hand, I pause to think how I can render in words a faint impression of the most inspiriting, the most fascinating human being that I have known.

I

It is nearly a quarter of a century since I first saw Stevenson. In the autumn of 1870, in company with a former schoolfellow, I was in the Hebrides. We had been wandering in the Long Island, as they name the outer archipelago, and our steamer, returning, called at Skye. At the pier of Portree, I think, a company came on board — "people of importance in their day," Edinburgh acquaintances, I suppose, who had accidentally met in Skye on various errands. At all events, they invaded our modest vessel with a loud sound of talk. Professor Blackie was among them, a famous figure that calls for no description; and a voluble, shaggy man, clad in homespun, with spectacles forward upon nose, who, it was whispered to us, was Mr Sam Bough, the Scottish Academician, a water-colour painter of some repute, who was to die in 1878. There were also several engineers of prominence. At the tail of this chatty, jesting little crowd of invaders came a youth of about my own age, whose appearance, for some mysterious reason, instantly attracted me. He was tall, preternaturally lean, with longish hair, and as restless and questing as a spaniel. The party from Portree fairly took possession of us; at meals they crowded around the captain, and we common tourists sat silent, below the salt. The stories of Blackie and Sam Bough were resonant. Meanwhile, I knew not why, I watched the plain, pale lad who took the lowest place in this privileged company.

The summer of 1870 remains in the memory of western Scotland as one of incomparable splendour. Our voyage, especially as evening drew on, was like an emperor's progress. We stayed on deck till the latest moment possible, and I occasionally watched the lean youth, busy and serviceable, with some of the little tricks with which we were later on to grow familiar — the advance with hand on hip, the sidewise bending of the head to listen. Meanwhile darkness overtook us, a wonderful halo of moonlight swam up over Glenelg, the indigo of the peaks of the Cuchullins faded into the general blue night. I went below, but was presently aware of some change of course, and then of an unexpected stoppage. I tore on deck, and found that we had left our track among the islands, and had steamed up a narrow and unvisited fiord of the mainland — I think Loch Nevis. The sight was curious and bewildering. We lay in a gorge of blackness, with only a strip of the blue moonlit sky overhead; in the dark a few laterns jumped about the shore, carried by agitated but unseen and soundless persons. As I leaned over the bulwarks, Stevenson was at my side, and he explained to me that we had come up this loch to take away to Glasgow a large party of emigrants driven from their homes in the interests of a deer-forest. As he spoke, a black mass became visible entering the vessel. Then, as we slipped of shore, the fact of their hopeless exile came home to these poor fugitives, and suddenly, through the absolute silence, there rose from them a wild kerning and wailing, reverberated by the cliffs of the loch, and at that strange place and hour infinitely poignant. When I came on deck

Anstruther, Fife

next morning, my unnamed friend was gone. He had put off with the engineers to visit some remote lighthouse of the Hebrides.

This early glimpse of Stevenson is a delightful memory to me. When we met next, not only did I instantly recall him, but, what was stranger, he remembered me. This voyage in the *Clansman* was often mentioned between us, and it has received for me a sort of consecration from the fact that in the very last letter that Louis wrote, finished on the day of his death, he made a reference to it.

II

In the very touching "Recollections" which our friend Mr Andrew Lang has published, he says: "I shall not deny that my first impression [of Stevenson] was not wholly favourable." I remember, too, that John Adding-ton Symonds was not pleased at first. It only shows how different are our moods. I must confess that in my case the invading army simply walked up and took the fort by storm. It was in 1877, or late in 1876, that I was presented to Stevenson, at the old Savile club, by Mr Sidney Colvin, who thereupon left us to our devices. We went downstairs and lunched together, and then we adjourned to the smoking-room. As twilight came on I tore myself away, but Stevenson walked with me across Hyde Park, and nearly to my house. He had an engagement, and so had I, but I walked a mile or two back with him. The fountains of talk had been unsealed, and they drowned the conventions. I came home dazzled with my new friend, saying, as Constance does of Arthur, "Was ever such a gracious creature born?" That imprssion of ineffable mental charm was formed at the first moment of acquaintance, and it never lessened or became modified. Stevenson's rapidity in the sympathetic interchange of ideas was, doubtless, the source of it. He has been described as an "egotist," but I challenge the description. If ever there was an altruist, it was Louis Stevenson; he seemed to feign an interest in himself merely to stimulate you to be liberal in your confidences.*

Those who have written about him from later impressions than those of which I speak seem to me to give insufficient prominence to the gaiety of Stevenson. It was his cardinal quality in those early days. A childlike mirth leaped and danced in him; he seemed to skip upon the hills of life. He was simply bubbling with quips and jests; his inherent earnestness or passion about abstract things was incessantly relieved by jocosity; and when he had built one of his intellectual castles in the sand, a wave of humour was certain to sweep in and destroy it. I cannot, for the life of me, recall any of his jokes; and written down in cold blood, they might not be funny if I did. They were not wit so much as humanity, the many-sided outlook upon life. I am anxious that his laughter-loving mood should not be forgotten, because later on it was partly, but I think never wholly, quenched by ill health, responsibility, and the advance of years. He was often, in the old days, excessively and delightfully silly — silly with the silliness of an inspired schoolboy; and I am afraid that our laughter sometimes sounded ill in the ears of age.

A pathos was given to his gaiety by the fragility of his health. He was never well, all the years I knew him; and we looked upon his life as hanging by the frailest tenure. As he never complained or maundered, this, no doubt — though we were not aware of it — added to the charm of his presence. He was so bright and keen and witty, and any week he might die. No one, certainly, conceived it possible that he could reach his forty-fifth year. In 1879 his health visibly began to run lower, and he used to bury himself in lonely Scotch and French places, "tinkering himself with solitude," as he used to say.

My experience of Stevenson during these first years was confined to London, upon which he would make sudden piratical descents, staying for a few days or weeks, and melting into air again. He was much at my house; and it must be told that my wife and I, as young married people, had possessed ourselves of a house too large for our slender means immediately to furnish. The one person who thoroughly approved of our great, bare, absurd drawing-room was Louis, who very earnestly dealt with us on the immorality of chairs and tables, and desired us to sit always, as he delighted to sit, upon hassocks on the floor. Nevertheless, as arm-chairs and settees straggled into existence, he handsomely consented to use them, although never in the usual way, but with his legs thrown sideways over the arms of them, or the head of a sofa treated as a perch. In particular, a certain shelf, with cupboards below, attached to a bookcase, is worn with the person of Stevenson, who would spend half an evening while passionately discussing some great question of morality or literature, leaping sidewise in a seated posture to the length of this shelf, and then back again. He was eminently peripatetic, too, and never better company than walking in the street, this exercise seeming to inflame his fancy. But his most habitual dwellingplace in the London of those days was the Savile Club, then lodged in an inconvenient but very friendly house in Savile Row. Louis pervaded the club; he was its most affable and chatty member; and he lifted it, by the ingenuity of his incessant dialectic, to the level of a sort of humorous Academe or Mouseion.

At this time he must not be thought of as a successful author. A very few of us were convinced of his genius; but with the exception of Mr Leslie Stephen, nobody of editorial status was sure of it. I remember the publication of *An Inland Voyage* in 1878, and the inability of the critics and the public to see anything unusual in it.

Stevenson was not without a good deal of innocent oddity in his dress. When I try to conjure up his figure, I can see only a slight, lean lad, in a suit of blue sea-cloth, a black shirt, and a wisp of yellow carpet that did duty for a necktie. This was long his attire, persevered in to the anguish of his more conventional acquaintances. I have a ludicrous memory of going, in 1878, to buy him a new hat, in company with Mr Lang, the thing then upon his head having lost the semblance of a human article of dress.

*This continued to be his characteristic to the last. Thus he described an interview he had in Sydney with some man formerly connected with the "black-birding" trade, by saying: "He was very shy at first, and it was not till I told him of a good many of my escapades that I could get him to thaw, and then he poured it all out. I have always found that the best way of getting people to be confidential."

Erraid

Aided by a very civil shopman, we suggested several hats and caps, and Louis at first seemed interested; but having presently hit upon one which appeared to us pleasing and decorous, we turned for a moment to inquire the price. We turned back, and found that Louis had fled, the idea of parting with the shapeless object having proved too painful to be entertained. By the way, Mr Lang will pardon me if I tell, in exacter detail, a story of his. It was immediately after the adventure with the hat that, not having quite enough money to take him from London to Edinburgh, third class, he proposed to the railway clerk to throw in a copy of Mr Swinburne's *Queen-Mother and Rosamund*. The offer was refused with scorn, although the book was of the first edition, and even then worth more than the cost of a whole ticket.

Stevensons's pity was a very marked quality, and it extended to beggars, which is, I think, to go too far. His optimism, however, suffered a rude shock in South Audley Street one summer afternoon. We met a stalwart beggar, whom I refused to aid. Louis, however, wavered, and finally handed him sixpence. The man pocketed the coin, forbore to thank his benefactor, but, fixing his eye on me, said, in a loud voice, "And what is the other little gentleman going to give me?" "In future," Louis said, as we strode coldly on, "*I* shall be 'the other little gentleman'."

In those early days he suffered many indignities on account of his extreme youthfulness of appearance and absence of self-assertion. He was at Inverness — being five or six and twenty at the time — and had taken a room in a hotel. Coming back about dinner-time, he asked the hour of table d'hôte, whereupon the landlady said, in a motherly way: "Oh, I knew you wouldn't like to sit in there among the grown-up people, so I've had a place put for you in the bar." There was a frolic at the Royal Hotel, Bathgate, in the summer of 1879. Louis was lunching alone, and the maid, considering him a negligible quantity, came and leaned out of the window. This outrage on the proprieties was so stinging that Louis at length made free to ask her, with irony, what she was doing there. "I'm looking for my lad," she replied. "Is that he?" asked Stevenson, with a keener sarcasm. "Weel, I've been lookin' for him a' my life, and I've never seen him yet'" was the response. Louis was disarmed at once, and wrote her on the spot some beautiful verses in the vernacular. "They're no bad for a beginner," she was kind enough to say when she had read them.

The year 1879 was a dark one in the life of Louis. He had formed a conviction that it was his duty to go out to the extreme west of the United States, while his family and the inner circle of his friends were equally certain that it was neither needful or expedient that he should make this journey. As it turned out, they were wrong, and he was right; but in the circumstances their opinion seemed the only correct one. His health was particularly bad, and he was ordered, not West, but South. The expedition, which he has partly described in *The Amateur Emigrant* and *Across the Plains*, was taken, therefore, in violent opposition to all those whom he left in England and Scotland; and this accounts for the mode in which it was taken. He did not choose to ask for money to be spent in going to California, and it was hoped that the withdrawal of supplies would make the voyage impossible. But Louis, bringing to the front a streak of iron obstinancy which lay hidden somewhere in his gentle nature, scraped together enough to secure him a steerage passage across the Atlantic.

The day before he started he spent with my wife and me — a day of stormy agitation, an April day of rain-clouds and sunshine; for it was not in Louis to remain long in any mood. I seem to see him now, pacing the room, a cigarette spinning in his wasted fingers. To the last we were trying to dissuade him from what seemed to us the maddest of enterprises. He was so ill that I did not like to leave him, and at night — it was midsummer weather — we walked down into town together. We were by this time, I suppose, in a pretty hysterical state of mind, and as we went through Berkeley Square, in mournful discussion of the future, Louis suddenly proposed that we should visit the so-called "Haunted House," which then occupied the newspapers. The square was quiet in the decency of a Sunday evening. We found the house, and one of us boldly knocked at the door. There was no answer and no sound, and we jeered upon the door-step; but suddenly we were both aware of a pale face — a phantasm in the dusk — gazing down upon us from a surprising height. It was the caretaker, I suppose, mounted upon a flight of steps: but terror gripped us at the heart, and we fled with footsteps as precipitate as those of schoolboys caught in an orchard. I think that ghostly face in Berkeley Square must have been Louis's latest European impression for many months.

III

All the world now knows, through the two books which I have named, what immediately happened. Presently letters began to arrive, and in one from Monterey, written early in October 1879, he told me of what was probably the nearest approach of death that ever came until the end, fifteen years later. I do not think it is generally known, even in the inner circle of his friends, that in September of that year he was violently ill, alone, at an Angora-goat ranch in the Santa Lucia Mountains. "I scarcely slept or ate or thought for four days," he said. "Two nights I lay out under a tree, in a sort of stupor, doing nothing but fetch water for myself and horse, light a fire and make coffee, and all night awake hearing the goat-bells ringing and the tree-toads singing, when each new noise was enough to set me mad." Then an old frontiersman, a mighty hunter of bears, came round, and tenderly nursed him through his attack. "By all rule this should have been my death; but after a while my spirit got up again in a divine frenzy, and has since kicked and spurred my vile body forward with great emphasis and success."

Late in the winter of 1879, with renewed happiness and calm of life, and also under the spur of a need of money, he wrote with much assiduity. Among other things, he composed at Monterey the earliest of his novels, a book called *A Vendetta in the West*, the manuscript of which seems to have disappeared. Perhaps we need not regret it; for, so he declared to me, "It was about as bad as Ouida, but not quite, for it was not so eloquent." He had made a great mystery of his whereabouts; indeed, for several months no one was to know what had become of him, and his letters were to be considered secret. At length, in writing from Monterey, on November 15, 1879, he removed the embargo: "That I am in California may now be published to the brethren." In the summer of the next year, after a winter of very serious ill health, during which more than once he seemed on the brink of galloping consumption, he returned to England. He had married in California a charming lady whom we all soon learned to regard as the most appropriate and helpful companion that Louis could possibly have secured. On October 8, 1880 — a memorable day — he made his first appearance in London since his American exile. A post-card from Edinburgh had summoned me to "appoint with an appointment" certain particular friends; "and let us once again," Louis wrote, "lunch together in the Savile Halls." Mr Lang and Mr Walter Pollock, and, I think, Mr Henley, graced the occasion, and the club cellar produced a bottle of Chambertin of quite uncommon merit. Louis, I may explain, had a peculiar passion for Burgundy, which he esteemed the wine of highest possibilities in the whole Bacchic order; and I have often known him descant on a Pommard or a Montrachet in terms so exquisite that the listeners could scarcely taste the wine itself.

Davos-Platz was now prescribed for the rickety lungs; and late in that year Louis and his wife took up their abode there, at the Hotel Buol, he carrying with him a note from me recommending him to the care of John Addington Symonds. Not at first, but presently and on the whole, these two men, so singular in the generation, so unique and so unlike, "hit it off," as people say, and were an intellectual solace to each other; but their real friendship did not begin till a later year. I remember

Stevenson saying to me next spring that to be much with Symonds was to "adventure in a thornwood." It was at Davos, this winter of 1880, that Stevenson took up the study of Hazlitt, having found a publisher who was willing to bring out a critical and biographical memoir. This scheme occupied a great part of Louis's attention, but was eventually dropped; for the further he progressed in the investigation of Hazlitt's character the less he liked it, and the squalid *Liber Amoris* gave the *coup de grâce*. He did not know what he would be at. His vocation was not yet apparent to him. He talked of writing on craniology and the botany of the Alps. The unwritten books of Stevenson will one day attract the scholiast, who will endeavour, perhaps, to reconstruct them from the references to them in his correspondence. It may, therefore, be permissible to record here that he was long proposing to write a life of the Duke of Wellington, for which he made some considerable collections. This was even advertised as "in preparation," on several occasions, from 1885 until 1887, but was ultimately abandoned. I remember his telling me that he intended to give emphasis to the "humour" of Wellington.

In June, 1881, we saw him again; but he passed rapidly through London to a cottage at Pitlochry in Perthshire. He had lost his hold on town. "London," he wrote me, "now chiefly means to me Colvin and Henley, Leslie Stephen and you." He was now coursing a fresh literary hare, and set Mr Austin Dobson, Mr Saintsbury, and me busily hunting out facts about Jean Cavalier, the romantic eighteenth-century adventurer, whose life he fancied that he would write. His thoughts had recurred, in fact, to Scottish history; and he suddenly determined to do what seemed rather a mad thing — namely, to stand for the Edinburgh professorship of history, then just vacant. We were all whipped up for testimonials, and a little pamphlet exists, in a pearl-grey cover — the despair of bibliophiles — in which he had a strange assortment of his friends set forth his claims. These required nimble treatment, since, to put it plainly, it was impossible to say that he had any. His appeal was treated by the advocates, who were the electing body, with scant consideration, and some worthy gentleman was elected. The round Louis was well out of such a square hole as a chair in a university.

Braemar Cottage

But something better was at hand. It was now, and in the peace of the Highlands, that Louis set out to become a popular writer. The fine art of "booming" had not then been introduced, nor the race of those who week by week discover coveys of fresh geniuses. Although Stevenson, in a sporadic way, had written much that was delightful, and that will last, he was yet — now at the close of his thirty-first year — by no means successful. The income he made by his pen was still ridiculously small; and Mr John

Morley, amazing as it sounds today, had just refused to give him a book to write in the *English Men of Letters* series, on the ground of his obscurity as an author. All this was to be changed, and the book that was to do it was even now upon the stocks. In August the Stevensons moved to a house in Braemar — a place, as Louis said, "patronised by the royalty of the Sister Kingdoms — Victoria and the Cairngorms, sir, honouring that countryside by their conjunct presence." Hither I was invited, and here I paid an ever memorable visit. The house, as Louis was careful to instruct me, was entitled "The Cottage, late the late Miss McGregor's, Castleton of Braemar"; and thus I obediently addressed my letters until Louis remarked that "the reference to a deceased Highland lady, tending as it does to foster unavailing sorrow, may be with advantage omitted from the address."

To the Cottage, therefore, heedless of the manes of the late Miss McGregor, I proceeded in the most violent storm of hail and rain that even Aberdeenshire can produce in August, and found Louis as frail as a ghost, indeed, but better than I expected. He had adopted a trick of stretching his thin limbs over the back of a wicker sofa, which gave him an extraordinary resemblance to that quaint insect, the praying mantis; but it was a mercy to find him out of bed at all. Among the many attractions of the Cottage, the presence of Mr Thomas Stevenson — Louis's father — must not be omitted. He was then a singularly charming and vigorous personality, indignantly hovering at the borders of old age ("Sixty-three, sir, this year; and, deuce take it! am I to be called 'an old gentleman' by a cab-driver in the streets of Aberdeen?") and, to my gratitude and delight, my companion in long morning walks. The detestable weather presently brought all the other members of the household to their beds, and Louis in particular became a wreck. However, it was a wreck that floated every day at nightfall; for at the worst he was able to come downstairs to dinner and spend the evening with us.

We passed the days with regularity. After breakfast I went to Louis's bedroom, where he sat up in bed, with dark, flashing eyes and ruffled hair, and we played chess on the coverlet. Not a word passed, for he was strictly forbidden to speak in the early part of the day. As soon as he felt tired — often in the middle of a game — he would rap with peremptory knuckles on the board as a signal to stop, and then Mrs Stevenson or I would arrange his writing materials on the bed. Then I would see no more of him till dinner-time, when he would appear, smiling and voluble, the horrid bar of speechlessness having been let down. Then every night, after dinner, he would read us what he had written during the day. I find in a note to my wife, dated September 3, 1881: "Louis has been writing, all the time I have been here, a novel of pirates and hidden treasure, in the highest degree exciting. He reads it to us every night, chapter by chapter." This, of course, was *Treasure Island*, about the composition of which, long afterward, in Samoa, he wrote an account in some parts of which I think that his memory played him false. I look back to no keener intellectual pleasure than those cold nights at Braemar, with the sleet howling outside, and Louis reading his budding romance by the lamplight, emphasising the purpler passages with lifted voice and gesticulating finger.

IV

Hardly had I left the Cottage than the harsh and damp climate of Aberdeenshire was felt to be rapidly destroying Louis, and he and his wife fled for Davos. Before the end of October they were ensconced there in a fairly comfortable châlet. Here Louis and his step-son amused themselves by setting up a hand-press, which Mr Osbourne worked, and for which Louis provided the literary material. Four or five laborious little publications were put forth, some of them illustrated by the daring hand of Stevenson himself. He complained to me that Mr Osbourne was a very ungenerous publisher — "one penny a cut, and one halfpenny a set of verses! What do you say to that for Grub Street?" These little diversions were brought to a close by the printer-publisher breaking, at one fell swoop, the press and his own finger. The little "Davos Press" issues now fetch extravagant prices, which would have filled author and printer with amazement. About this time Louis and I had a good deal of correspondence about a work which he had proposed that we should undertake in collaboration — a retelling, in choice literary form, of the most picturesque murder cases of the last hundred years. We were to visit the scenes of these crimes, and turn over the evidence. The great thing, Louis said, was not to begin to write until we were thoroughly alarmed. "These things must be done, my boy, under the very shudder of the goose-flesh." We were to begin with the "Story of the Red Barn," which indeed is a tale pre-eminently worthy to be retold by Stevenson. But the scheme never came off, and is another of the dead leaves in his Vallombrosa.

We saw him in London again, for a few days, in October 1882; but this was a melancholy period. For eight months at the close of that year and the beginning of 1883 he was capable of no mental exertion. He was in the depths of languor, and in nightly apprehension of a fresh attack. He slept excessively, and gave humorous accounts of the drowsiness that hung upon him, addressing his notes as "from the Arms of Porpus" (Morpheus) and "at the Sign of the Poppy." No climate seemed to relieve him, and so, in the autumn of 1882, a bold experiment was tried. As the snows of Davos were of no avail, the hot, damp airs of Hyères should be essayed. I am inclined to dwell in some fulness on the year he spent at Hyères, because, curiously enough, it was not so much as mentioned, to my knowledge, by any of the writers of obituary notices at Stevenson's death. It takes, nevertheless, a prominent place in his life's history, for his removal thither marked a sudden and brilliant, though only temporary, revival in his health and spirits. Some of his best work, too, was written at Hyères, and one might say that fame first found him in this warm corner of southern France.

The house at Hyères was called "La Solitude." It stood in a paradise of roses and aloes, fig-marigolds and olives. It had delectable and even, so Louis declared, "sub-celestial" views over a plain bounded by "certain mountains as graceful as Apollo, as severe as Zeus"; and at first the hot mistral, which blew and burned where it blew, seemed the only drawback. Not a few of the best poems in the *Underwoods* reflect the ecstasy of convalescence under the skies and perfumes of La Solitude. By the summer Louis could report "good health of a radiant order." It was while he was at Hyères that Stevenson first directly addressed an American audience, and I may record that, in September 1883, he told me to "beg Gilder your prettiest for a gentleman in pecuniary sloughs." Mr Gilder was quite alive to the importance of securing such a contributor, although when the Amateur Emigrant had entered the office of *The Century Magazine* in 1879 he had been very civilly but coldly shown the door. (I must be allowed to tease my good friends in Union Square by recording that fact!) Mr Gilder asked for fiction, but received instead *The Silverado Squatters*, which duly appeared in the magazine.

It was also arranged that Stevenson should make an ascent of the Rhône for *The Century*, and Mr Joseph

Lloyd Osbourne

Pennell was to accompany him to make sketches for the magazine. But Stevenson's health failed again: the sudden death of a very dear old friend was a painful shock to him, and the winter of that year was not propitious. Abruptly, however, in January 1884, another crisis came. He went to Nice, where he was thought to be dying. He saw no letters; all his business was kindly taken charge of by Mr Henley; and again, for a long time, he passed beneath the penumbra of steady languor and infirmity. When it is known how constantly he suffered, how brief and flickering were the intervals of comparative health, it cannot but add to the impression of his radiant fortitude through all these trials, and of his persistent employment of all his lucid moments. It was pitiful, and yet at the same time very inspiriting, to see a creature so feeble and so ill equipped for the struggle bear himself so smilingly and so manfully through all his afflictions. There can be no doubt, however, that this latest breakdown vitally affected his spirits. He was never, after this, quite the gay child of genius that he had previously been. Something of a graver cast became natural to his thoughts; he had seen Death in the cave. And now for the first time we traced a new note in his writings — the note of "Pulvis et Umbra."

After 1883 my personal memories of Stevenson become very casual. In November 1884, he was settled at Bournemouth, in a villa called Bonallie Towers, and there he stayed until, in March 1885, he took a house of his own, which, in pious memory of his grandfather, he named Skerryvore. In the preceding winter, when I was going to America to lecture, he was particularly anxious that I should lay at the feet of Mr Frank R. Stockton his homage, couched in the following lines:

My Stockton if I failed to like
It were a sheer depravity;
For I went down with the "Thomas Hyke,"
And up with the "Negative Gravity."

He adored these tales of Mr Stockton's, a taste which must be shared by all good men. To my constant sorrow, I was never able to go to Bournemouth during the years he lived there. It has been described to me, by those who were more fortunate, as a pleasure that was apt to tantalize and evade the visitor, so constantly was the invalid unable, at the last, to see the friend who had travelled a hundred miles to speak with him. It was therefore during his visits to London, infrequent as these were, that we saw him at his best, for these were at moments of unusual recovery. He generally lodged at what he called the "Monument," this being his title for Mr Colvin's house, a wing of the vast structure of the British Museum. I recall an occasion on which Louis dined with us (March 1886), because of the startling interest in the art of strategy which he had developed — an interest which delayed the meal with arrangements of

serried bottles counter-scarped and lines of cruets drawn up on horseback ready to charge. So infectious was his enthusiasm that we forgot our hunger, and hung over the embattled table-cloth, easily persuaded to agree with him that neither poetry nor the plastic arts could compete for a moment with "the finished conduct, sir, of a large body of men in face of the enemy."

It was a little later that he took up the practice of modelling clay figures as he sat up in bed. Some of these compositions — which needed, perhaps, his eloquent commentary to convey their full effect to the spectator — were not without a measure of skill of design. I recollect his saying, with extreme gravity, "I am in sculpture what Mr Watts is in painting. We are both of us pre-occupied with moral and abstract ideas." I wonder whether any one has preserved specimens of these allegorical groups of clay.

The last time I had the happiness of seeing Stevenson was on Sunday, August 21, 1887. He had been brought up from Bournemouth the day before in a wretched condition of health, and was lodged in a private hotel in Finsbury Circus, in the City, ready to be easily moved to a steamer in the Thames on the morrow. I was warned, in a note, of his passage through town, and of the uncertainty whether he could be seen. On the chance, I went over early on the 21st, and, very happily for me, he had a fair night, and could see me for an hour or two. No one else but Mrs Stevenson was with him. His position was one which might have daunted any man's spirit, doomed to exile, in miserable health, starting vaguely across the Atlantic, with all his domestic interests rooted up, and with no notion where, or if at all, they should be replanted. If ever a man of imagination could be excused for repining, it was now.

But Louis showed no white feather. He was radiantly humorous and romantic. It was church time, and there was some talk of my witnessing his will, which I could not do, because there could be found no other reputable witness, the whole crew of the hotel being at church. This set Louis off on a splendid dream of romance. "This," he said, "is the way in which our valuable city hotels — packed, doubtless, with rich object of jewellery — are deserted on a Sunday morning. Some bold piratical fellow, defying the spirit of Sabbatarianism, might make a

Hawes Inn, South Queensferry

handsome revenue by sacking the derelict hotels between the hours of ten and twelve. One hotel a week would suffice to enable such a man to retire into private life within the space of a year. A mask might, perhaps, be worn for the mere fancy of the thing, and to terrify kitchen-maids, but no real disguise would be needful to an enterprise that would require nothing but a brave heart and a careful study of the City Postal Directory." He spoke of the matter with so much fire and gallantry that I blushed for the youth of England and its lack of manly enterprise. No one ever could describe preposterous conduct with such a convincing air as Louis could. Common sense was positively humbled in his presence.

The volume of his poems called *Underwoods* had just appeared, and he inscribed a copy of it to me in the words "at Todgers', as ever was, *chez Todgers*, Pecksniff street."

The only new book he seemed to wish to carry away with him was Mr Hardy's beautiful romance, *The Woodlanders*, which we had to scour London that Sunday afternoon to get hold of. In the evening Mr Colvin and I each returned to "Todgers'" with the three volumes, borrowed or stolen somewhere, and wrapped up for the voyage next day. And so the following morning, in an extraordinary vessel called the *Ludgate Hill* — as though in compliment to Mr Stockton's genius — and carrying, besides the Stevensons, a cargo of stallions and monkeys, Mr and Mrs Stevenson and Mr Lloyd Osbourne steamed down the Thames in search of health across the Atlantic and the Pacific. The horses, Louis declared, protruded their noses in an unmannerly way between the passengers at dinner, and the poor little grey monkeys, giving up life for a bad job on board that strange, heaving cage, died by dozens, and were flung contemptuously out into the ocean. The strangest voyage, however, some time comes to an end, and Louis landed in America. He was never to cross the Atlantic again; and for those who loved him in Europe he had already journeyed more than half-way to another world.

V

It is impossible to deal, however lightly, with the personal qualities of Robert Louis Stevenson without dwelling on the extreme beauty of his character. In looking back over the twenty years in which I knew him, I feel that, since he was eminently human, I ought to recall his faults, but I protest that I can remember none. Perhaps the nearest approach to a fault was a certain want of discretion, always founded on a wish to make people understand each other, but not exactly according to wisdom. I recollect that he once embroiled me for a moment with John Addington Symonds in a manner altogether bloodthirsty and ridiculous, so that we both fell upon him and rended him. This little weakness is really the blackest crime I can lay to his charge. And on the other side, what courage, what love, what an indomitable spirit, what a melting pity! He had none of the sordid errors of the little man who writes — no sick ambition, no envy of others, no exaggeration of the value of this ephemeral trick of scribbling. He was eager to help

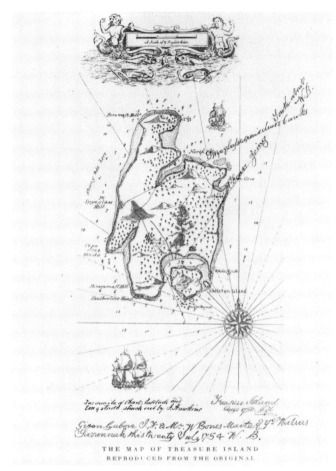

THE MAP OF TREASURE ISLAND
REPRODUCED FROM THE ORIGINAL

Map for *Treasure Island*

his fellows, ready to take a second place, with great difficulty offended, by the least show of repentance perfectly appeased.

Quite early in his career he adjusted himself to the inevitable sense of physical failure. He threw away from him all the useless impediments: he sat loosely in the saddle of life. Many men who get such a warning as he got take up something to lean against; according to their education or temperament, they support their maimed existence on religion, or on cynical indifference, or on some mania of the collector or the *dilettante*. Stevenson did none of these things. He determined to make the sanest and most genial use of so much of life as was left him. As any one who reads his books can see, he had a deep strain of natural religion; but he kept it to himself; he made no hysterical or ostentatious use of it.

Looking back at the past, one recalls a trait that had its significance, though one missed its meaning then. He was careful, as I have hardly known any other man to be, not to allow himself to be burdened by the weight of material things. It was quite a jest with us that he never acquired any possessions. In the midst of those who produced books, pictures, prints, bric-à-brac, none of these things ever stuck to Stevenson. There are some deep-sea creatures, the early part of whose life is spent dancing through the waters; at length some sucker or tentacle touches a rock, adheres, pulls down more tentacles, until the creature is caught there, stationary for the remainder of its existence. So it happens to men, and Stevenson's friends, one after another, caught the ground with a house, a fixed employment, a "stake in life"; he alone kept dancing in the free element, unattached. I remember his saying to me that if ever he had a garden he should like it to be empty, just a space to walk and talk in, with no flowers to need a gardener nor fine lawns that had to be mown. Just a fragment of the bare world to move in, that was all Stevenson asked for. And we who gathered possessions around us — a little library of rare books, a little gallery of drawings or bronzes — he mocked us with his goblin laughter; it was only so much more luggage to carry on the march, he said, so much more to strain the arms and bend the back.

Stevenson thought, as we all must think, that literature is a delightful profession, a primrose path. I remember his once saying so to me, and then he turned, with the brimming look in his lustrous eyes and the tremulous smile on his lips, and added, "But it is not all primroses, some of it is brambly, and most of it uphill." He knew — no one better — how the hill catches the breath and how the brambles tear the face and hands; but he pushed strenuously, serenely on, searching for new paths, struggling to get up into the light and air.

One reason why it was difficult to be certain that Stevenson had reached his utmost in any direction was what I will call, for want of a better phrase, the *energetic modesty* of his nature. He was never satisfied with himself, yet never cast down. There are two dangers that beset the artist — the one is being pleased with what he has done, and the other being dejected with it. Stevenson, more than any other man whom I have known, steered the middle course. He never conceived that he had achieved a great success, but he never lost hope that by taking pains he might yet do so. Twelve years ago, when he was beginning to write that curious and fascinating book, *Prince Otto*, he wrote to me describing the mood in which one should go about one's work — golden words, which I have never forgotten. "One should strain," he said, "and then play, strain again, and play again. The strain is for us, it educates; the play is for the reader, and pleases. In moments of effort one learns to do the easy things that people like."

He learned that which he desired, and he gained more than he hoped for. He became the most exquisite English writer of his generation; yet those who lived close to him are apt to think less of this than of the fact that he was the most unselfish and the most lovable of human beings.

I Enter R. L. S.

WILL LOW

I have spoken of the plaster lion which guarded the doorway leading to the painters' studios at "eighty-one." Since his brief hour of glory in some long-forgotten Salon exhibition the noble animal had encountered many vicissitudes, and suffered such indignity at the hands of a lawless generation, in his long career as sentinel at our door. Bereft of his tail, with pencilled mustaches and many scrawled inscriptions covering him, it was left to my ingenious friend Bob[1] to discover that, by beating this king of beasts with his cane, the reverberations of his hollow plaster interior made an excellent substitute for a gong. This my friend put to use, rather than climb the stairs and knock at my door, when he desired to communicate with me. Thus summoned one spring evening in 1875 to my window, I looked down to find Bob arrayed for the street, intent upon a walk and a dinner afterward somewhere on the heights of Montmartre, where we seldom ventured, for which he desired my company.

Descending to the courtyard I joined him, and in passing we paused at the porter's lodge to inquire for letters. There was one for Bob which he tore open, and after scanning it passed to me, saying, "Louis is coming over." I read the brief note; it was the first time I saw the handwriting which was to become so familiar to me and by whose medium the world was to gain so greatly. I fancy I can see it yet, the blue-gray paper with the imprint of the Savile Club in London, the few scrawled words to the effect that the writer was "seedy," that the weather was bad in London, and that he would arrive the next morning in Paris to seek sunshine and rest, and at the end the three initials R. L. S. which now are known the world over.

I had heard much of this cousin, of the life which Bob and he had led in Edinburgh, where their revolt against the overstrict conventionality of that famous town had

been flavoured with the zest of forbidden fruit. I had heard in detail of escapades innocent enough, the outcome of boyish spirits, in which both had shared, and of which Bob, philosophically enough, had borne the blame of leading the younger cousin into mischief. I had also heard that Louis was "going in" for literature, but this had not interested me particularly, for in those days we were all "going in" for one thing or the other; and so long as it was not banking, commerce, politics, or other unworthy or material pursuits it merely seemed the normal and proper function of life. I had heard enough, however, aided by my hearty affection for my friend Bob, to be keenly interested in the advent of the cousin, and I awaited the morrow with some impatience, for it was at once decided that we would meet the newcomer on his arrival at the St. Lazare station.

The morrow dawned, one of those days which fickle Paris gives in the spring to atone for her many climatic misdeeds of the winter. A filmy sky, the sunshine softly veiled, the trees in the fresh glory of their new attire, and the life of the streets partaking of the joyousness of the *renouveau*, as the old French calendars name their spring. It was a good day to undertake anything, better still to journey across the beautiful city, loitering on the bridges or through the courtyard of the Louvre and, best of all, to meet a new friend: to add to one's life another link in the chain of friendship, the most enduring of human ties.

At the appointed hour there descended from the Calais train a youth "unspeakably slight," with the face now familiar to us, the eyes widely spaced, a nose slightly aquiline and delicately modelled, the high cheek bones of the Scot; a face which in repose was not, I fancy, unlike that of many of his former comrades in his native town. It was not a handsome face until he spoke, and then I can hardly imagine that any could deny the appeal of the vivacious eyes, the humour or pathos of the mobile mouth, with its lurking suggestion of the great god Pan at times, or fail to realize that here was one so evidently

---

[1] R.A.M. Stevenson, Louis Stevenson's cousin.

Glencorse Churchyard

touched with genius that the higher beauty of the soul was his.

The appearance and the sense of youth he kept through life, though this was perhaps more discernible in conversation with him than from the published portraits. An early one of these from a photograph taken in California, though some years later than our first meeting, preserves much the same aspect as that he had when he stepped from the Calais train on the memorable spring-time morning in 1875.

One other detail of personal appearance I mention, for we hear much in his latter life of his long black hair. His hair never was black, though it grew darker with advancing years and became brown of the deepest hue, but at the time of our first meeting and for some years later it was very light, almost of the sandy tint we are wont to associate with his countrymen. In proof of this I have a little colour-sketch, painted in the autumn of '75, which shows him with his flaxen locks; "all that we have," as his wife once said sadly, "that will make people believe that Louis' hair was ever light."

Of his dress my memory is less vivid. He may have

worn a velvet coat or a knit jersey in guise of waistcoat; I have known him to do both at later periods, unconscious that for the boulevards at least his costume was less than suitable; but I aver nothing. Later he laughingly recalled that I appeared to him that morning in a frock coat and a smoking-cap; and if his recollection was correct — if I had, knowing that I was to meet one free from Gallic prejudice, temporarily resurrected my sealskin *toque*, which in any case was not a smoking-cap — it will be seen that my taste in dress was sufficiently eclectic to condone any lapse from strict conventionality on his part.

The formalities of introduction were soon over. The formalities of intercourse never weighed heavily upon us in those days, nor indeed with Louis in aftertime; his luggage was despatched to Lavenue's hotel, contiguous to the restaurant, and consequently near our studios, and light-handed and light-hearted we proceeded to retrace our steps across Paris.

And then began a flow of talk which, as I look back, seems to have been an irresistible current flowing through our lives, not only on this occasion but whenever, in Louis' frequent sojourn in France for the next few years, we three met together. Talk, even of the quality of which my two friends were past masters, is a light wine that can be neither bottled for preservation or decanted, and if I were able to here faithfully report the abundantly flowing discourse of that day, doubtless it would appear of no great import. There would still be lacking the atmosphere of spring in Paris, the growing interest of three sympathetic yet widely differing natures, and, above all, the brave outlook upon life from the vantage-ground of youth. For we were very young, Louis Stevenson three years my elder, and his cousin three years his senior, but our combined ages were scarcely more than the three score years and ten allotted to man in which to acquire wisdom.

Wisdom, therefore, we had not, but we had ideas and were not chary of their expression; we had insatiable curiosity upon all subjects pertaining to art and letters, and to life as well, though in the restricted sense in which, by representation, art sought the expression of life, or was in turn influenced by human conditions.

Hence it is no great loss that few of the many words uttered on this day of our first meeting have lived beyond their birth; but it was good to be out in pleasant sunshine, in the city kind above all others to our kind, to be at the threshold of our lives, and even the certainty, which probably we all felt that what we were saying was important, that possibly the whole course of art and letters was waiting expectantly for our decision before determining its final direction, may be pardoned us.

Again I must qualify my words. We had the strong, the ordinary, convictions of youth, but we had also some of its modesty. One who, like Louis, had such a hearty respect for his craft, so great a solicitude from the first to master his tools before essaying to use them, never, even when he had made himself master to a degree attained by few English men of letters, conceived his individual effort to be important. This, in the quasi-solitude in which he had lived in his native town, he had taught himself. As for the other two: if Paris teaches much that is worthy to the practitioners of art, she teaches nothing more worthy, nor more thoroughly, than the lesson that Art is long; that to reach the heights that others have attained, the route is stony and difficult.

Therefore, on that spring morning, we already carried as ballast to the clipper-ship of our speculative theories upon the inexhaustible subject of art the sobering conviction that our individual effort was but 'prentice work, and that before we could count as accepted workmen in our several crafts much water would run under the Bridge of Arts on its way to the sea.

Our wandering steps had brought us to that Pont des Arts which, bridging the Seine from the Louvre to the Institute, is most appropriately the only bridge in Paris over which you must walk; no easy progress in a carriage is possible for him who follows that path. Here we sat on a bench in the sun, looking up to where the boat-shaped Cité swims upon the current, bearing the proud towers of Notre Dame. To the left we could follow the long façade of the Louvre, and to the right stood the Institute where, as we know, forty antiquated gentlemen sat in judgement upon aesthetic France; a judgement which we were prepared to question, an institution we were equally prepared to overthrow; though to-day forty gentlemen, some of the same, still more antiquated, and others replacing those gone to their Academical reward, still continue to govern aesthetic France, while another generation of brash youths continues to question its judgments.

We sat basking in the sun for some time, talking of many things after the manner of the Walrus and the Carpenter, until, at the approach of noon, we discovered that we were hungry, and, forsaking the pathway of the Arts, came down to earth, hailed an open carriage and rode in state to Lavenue's. This was Louis Stevenson's first visit to the restaurant of our predilection of which he in turn became a votary; in his letters and his published works its name is often mentioned and its praises sounded. The mendacious divinity who presides over the bad quarter hour of payment — Rosalie-Fanny (or Fanny-Rosalie) — will to-day aver that she remembers the cousins well, and certainly for a number of years they were frequent visitors to her shrine.

This morning, in honour of the occasion, we had a better *déjeuner* than usual, and, scorning the *vin ordinaire*, we drank to our better acquaintance in an excellent Beaujolais-Fleury at two francs fifty centimes the bottle, a vintage of which Louis wrote to me four or five years later, after my return to the United States:

"Lavenue, hallowed be his name! Hallowed his old Fleury — of which you did not see — as I did — the glorious apotheosis; advanced on a Tuesday to three francs, on the Thursday to six, and on Friday swept off, holus-bolus, for the proprietor's private consumption. Well, we had the start of that proprietor. Many a good bottle came our way and was worthily made welcome."

Here after our lunch, with coffee and cigarettes we sat, as we did so often on later occasions, until four or five in the afternoon. Before, during and after the meal we talked, and here I was to encounter, for the first time, a whimsical instance of my new friend's sense of fitness in language. We were deep in a discussion about some detail or character of Balzac, the particular point we sought to elucidate I have forgotten, but at the time Bob and I were deep in the wonderful reconstitution of the life of France from Napoleon to Louis Phillipe which the master-romancer had fashioned, and Louis, we found, was no less interested than ourselves. Suddenly, without a note of warning, Louis changed from the language we had spoken up to that moment, which, of course, was our native English, to French. Now Bob spoke French somewhat hesitatingly, choosing his words with care but with excellent knowledge of the idiom; Louis' French was not unlike his cousin's; and mine, picked up in a more constant frequentation of French companions than is common among foreigners in Paris, was sufficiently fluent. I forbear to characterize our accents; having indeed, to this day reasons for avoiding that thorny subject in so far as I am personally concerned.

Up to the time of this change of language not one word of French had been spoken, and for all that Louis knew I might have been helpless in that polite tongue, but as we continued I soon realized that for our particular discussion of characters, events and of style, which were all French in essence, my new friend was not ill-inspired, and that we three English-speaking youths could better analyze the subject before us in French than in our native tongue. Speaking of this long after, I found that Louis had quite forgotten the incident, and I think it probable that at the time he was hardly conscious of it, his sense of the proper word and the fit phrase leading him into this excursion into a foreign language.

From Lavenue's we sought the garden of the Luxembourg, where we sat long into the twilight, taking our dinner somewhere near and adjourning to a café afterward. Here with our coffee a cordial, chartreuse or curaçoa was brought in a small decanter, accompanied by the usual small liqueur glasses; and here the impish extravagance of my new friend, which was at the bottom of so many of the youthful escapades in Edinburgh, and which, conducted with an enthusiasm worthy of more serious objects, had more than once caused dire prognostications of his future to be drawn, became manifest.

"I wonder," he said suddenly while sipping his cordial, "why this sort of thing is always served in such small glasses," and calling for an ordinary water glass, he half filled it with the cordial and drank it. I exclaimed in horror that it would make him ill, but, enjoying my surprise, he declared that it did not matter, because "I have come to Paris to rest and to-morrow I shall lie abed all day." This was the first reference to his feeling "seedy," which his letter had mentioned, and, indeed, throughout his life, except when it was forced upon him by actual physical prostration, beyond the precautions which he later learned to observe, there was no allusion to, no apparent realization of, his delicate condition. At this time, and during the three years that followed, I was never conscious that he was more than a little less robust than most of us were.

Knowing him as intimately as I did, it was not until a much later time that I realized that his early sojourns in the South of France were in the quest of health. At Barbizon he was among the foremost in our long walks over the plains or in the forest of Fontainbleau, and in the summers of 1876-77 at Grez, where he led a semi-amphibious life, on and in the river Loing, he never seemd ill, and as youth is not solicitous on questions of health, it never occured to us that his slender frame encased a less robust constitution than that of others. "My illness is an incident outside of my life" was his watchword later, and I need not enlarge on his brave attitude in that respect.

At the close of this eventful day we sauntered leisurely up the Boulevard St. Michael, entering, for a few moments, the Bal Bullier, which we surveyed philosophically, as prudent youths taking their pleasure otherwise, and having small interest in the riotous scenes enacted there. Thence, descending the Boulevard Mont Parnasse, we escorted Louis to the door of his hostelry, where we left him, appointing a meeting for the following evening, in order that he might carry out his plan of resting through the day undisturbed.

At the appointed time he reappeared, feeling, he assured us, much refreshed, and the morning after the two cousins departed for Barbizon. I was urged to accompany them, but I was busy upon a picture which was to be my first offering to the Salon. Could I have foreseen the cruelty of the jury of admission some days later I should have foregone this exhibition of Spartan virtue and, accompanying my friends, would now be able to describe the first impression which the smiling plain and shady woods made on Stevenson; who for several years was to find in Fontainebleau and the adjoining villages of Barbizon and Grez fields for work and play, influential at the time, and to which, in pleasant memory, he often reverted, until the end came in the far South Seas.

II   Our Work, Our Play, and Our Thoughts

What was it that rendered our sojourn in Fontainebleau and its outlying villages so influential in our lives and of such compelling charm that, whenever after I met with Bob or Louis, we resumed our intercourse as though intervening time and the many accidents along the way were banished, and we were once more at the threshold of our life?

The common interest of our projected life-work was undoubtedly at the root of this close and enduring association, but probably the strongest factor was that, though of nationality so dissimilar, of early influences so completely disassociated, we were, for the first time and in common, enjoying the large liberty of thought and action that in France is vouchsafed to the children of the arts. This was to us as is the breath of life; for no matter how sympathetic a restrained circle may be in other lands to the embryonic artist, no such environment can replace his universal acceptance and the dignity of the position accorded him, which for so many centuries has made that country the *alma mater* of the arts.

We know with what little favour the chosen vocation of Louis Stevenson was regarded at home, and how he had been obliged to adopt a profession esteemed more respectable. His cousin, to whom Louis wrote a few months before his death, "You wouldn't imitate, hence you kept free — a wild dog outside the kennel," never forgot those early days in Edinburgh. Later in life, when writing of Velasquez, in explanation of the independence of the Spanish master's art, upspringing like a flower in the arid soil of "a bigoted and fantastically ceremonious court," he evidently reverts to his own experience. "Many old men, reared in the puritanical and hypocritical Edinburgh of the past, could tell you the private reactionary effect of that life of repression and humbug

Equator

upon a decent genuine man. That you may not think at all, or act for yourself, is to add the very zest of piracy to experiment in life and originality in thought. Where public profession is manifestly a lie and public manners a formal exaggeration, life becomes a chest with a false bottom which opens into a refuge for the kindlier, wiser, and more ardent among human beings."

These conditions had borne hard upon my friends, and though in many ways my earlier lot had been happier, the neophyte in art in the days of my youth in our newer country was a little considered and solitary figure — his survivor even to-day having no very definite place in our social fabric. Hence, with something of the joy of colts let out to pasture, we had embraced the wider horizon, and above all, the untrammeled liberty that was unquestionally accorded to our kind in the pleasant land of France.

In after years, according to the manners and customs of our several countries, we affronted existing conditions and each in our way became very respectable dray-horses; but when met together, some whiff of keener air from the plains of Fountainebleau blew our way, and the coltish spirit of our youth was reawakened.

Art and life were such synonymous terms with us, in those days, that to have as virtually our only associates men who, almost without exception, were devoted to some form of art, lent joy to existence — even when intimacy was foregone and the relations were purely formal. Their mere numbers, however, ensured enough variety of opinions to make the interchange of thought wholesome and to keep our minds active; while the prosecution of our actual work added the healthy influence of practice to theory.

There were few drones in this busy hive of art, but of these Louis was apparently the most consistent. We have learned since how many impressions of scenes and manner were garnered from this apparent idleness, and through what a formative period in his work he was passing at the time. But I never remember him withdrawing to the seclusion of his room on the plea of work to be done, or in the long afternoons spent in his company, while I was industriously "spoiling canvas," as with more truth than I imagined we were wont to say with facetious intent, can I recall him as busy with paper and pencil. Even the book, which was his frequent companion, was more than likely left unopened. On the other hand, it is with gratifying frequency that I find in his published works ideas and reflections born of that time, and in many instances phrases and incidents that bring back some special place in the forest, or the life that we lived at Barbizon, Grez, or Montigny-sur-Loing. Industrious idleness it was to him; for his mind was a treasure-house, where every addition to its store was carefully guarded against the day of need. Many incidents of our common experience, long forgotten by me, I have thus met in fresh guise in after years; and in most cases I imagine that it was his memory and not his notes that served him — at least of these last there was no visible evidence at the time.

Despite our intimacy we lived so much in the present, each day bringing its quota of fresh experience, that it was long after in interchange of reminiscent talk that I learned of his earlier life, of the days when he was "ordered South," and of the storm and stress of his adolescent years.

Though is was considered "good form" in our circle to expatiate at length upon the work that we were doing, and to display it on every occasion in the most unblushing manner, he was an exception to the rule; vague mention of the few things he had published reached our ears, but no copies of them were produced; and it was not until the summer of 1876 that I first saw his work printed — the essay entitled "Forest Notes" in the "Cornhill" for May of that year.

I remember now a slight feeling of disappointment as I read this first specimen of his work; a feeling perhaps akin to that expressed by a little girl, the daughter of a well-known writer in New York, to whom a copy of the "Child's Garden of Verses" had been given: "Huh, I don't think much of those verses; *I think things just like them myself.*"

We were living the life described in this essay; one passage recalls the sketch of mine that in colour is the "only proof we have that Louis's hair was ever light"; and, though it admirably stands the test of his own definition of the difference between the work of the amateur and that of the writer master of his craft, "never to put into two pages the matter of one," it nevertheless appeared to me at the time to be less than I expected from the impression that his conversation and the charm of his presence had created.

The charm of his presence was both appealing and imperative, and though for other friends — for Bob especially — the ties that bind young men together and lay the foundations for lifelong friendships were quite as strong, Louis, quite unconsciously, exercised a species of fascination whenever we were together. Fascination and charm are not qualities which Anglo-Saxon youths are prone to acknowledge, in manly avoidance of their supposedly feminizing effect, but it was undoubtedly this attractive power which R. L. S. held so strongly through life; and which, gentle though it may have been, held no trace of dependence or weakness, that led Edmund Gosse

Siron's Inn

to exclaim, when I chanced to meet him at a crowded reception in New York long before Stevenson had attained a trans-Atlantic reputation: "I am told that you are a friend of Louis Stevenson. Do you know any one in the world that you would better like to have walk in on us at the present moment?"

The charm, therefore, of the long afternoons spent with him in the woods, his book thrown aside, the long fingers twisting cigarettes of thread-like dimensions, — I have never known any one to roll so thin a cigarette as Stevenson, — and the constant flow of talk and interchange of thought come back to me like the opening chapters of a book, which one has perused with increasing delight, only to find it at the end by "a wilful convulsion of brute nature" finished too soon.

This is the recollection of the time passed alone with him or when Bob was present; but, when our whole company was gathered together, the talk took a more turbulent course and generally with good humour, but always with the "engaging frankness of youth," much banter was tossed to and fro. One witticism recurs to me that afterward attained respectability in the staid columns of the "Saturday Review"; that was, I believe, first provoked by the indignant protest of the gallophile of our party, against the character of certain criticisms of the manners and customs of the land where we sojourned. "Don't mind him," drawled the insular critic, "he is *privately* a Frenchman."

As already described, the two Stevensons and the writer occasionally drifted out of the English-speaking circle and had experiences more tinged with the local colour of the village life. One such experience I should hestitate to write, perhaps, as it seems like taking a post humous revenge for the indiscretions of my friend, who did not scruple to portray an encounter that one may chance to have had with the seductive qualities of the wine of Roussilon in the pages of "The Wrecker," and then make plain its reference in the Epilogue addressed to me. As this other experience was, however, unique in my long frequentation of the society of R. L. S., it may figure here as a detail in my portrayal of the man.

One morning Siron took the three of us aside and explained that that evening a dinner was to be given by him in honour of the baptism of his first grandchild, and that, as it was manifestly impossible for him to invite all the sojourners at his inn, he had flatteringly chosen us from their number, and desired our presence at the dinner. We had, however, a previous engagement to pass the evening with our friend La Chèvre; but, seeing Siron's evident disappointment, we promised to come in later and assist in properly launching the innocent grandchild upon the troubled waves of life.

When, after a pleasant evening with our friends at the end of the village, and the customary supper washed down with some excellent white wine, we arrived at the scene of the baptismal dinner, the festivities were at their height. The table had been spread at one end of the long garden behind the hotel and some forty guests were present, including the proud parents, all the relations near or remote, and the chef and other servants of the hotel. Coffee had been served and song was in order, each of the guests in turn aiming to shine in sentimental or comic vein; the chef, already far gone in liquor, at once rising ready to burst into melody as each singer finished his contribution, and being as promptly suppressed. The proud father of the babe was one of the forest guards, an Alsatian, who, like so many of the sons of that unhappy province, had been given his choice after the annexation to leave his native province or remain and become subject of the hated German empire. He had chosen to remain French and had been rewarded with his post as one of the guardians of the forest. Our arrival only temporarily checked the flow of song, more wine was brought, many toasts were drunk, and, as the whole atmosphere seemd charged with the vapours of a Gargantuan repast plentifully liquefied by an abundance of the juice of the grape, it was not long before we three, ordinarily temperate youths, rose to the festival heights where our friends were enthroned. The muse was largely patriotic, the wounds of the late war were hardly healed, and the presence of one who had given up the hearths of his fathers at the call of patriotism, dictated the choice of the post-prandial *répertoire*. We heard thundered forth how at Reichshoffen death had closed up the ranks of the *cuirassiers*, and various other songs bewailing the sorrows of France and vowing vengeance on her enemies, when the forest guard rose precipitately and, with an embracing movement, drew the three of us into the cool recesses of the garden. Once there he turned, the tears streaming down his visage and cried: "Now, *Messieurs*, we will weep together for the sorrows of France!" After that my memory is somewhat confused, though I have a continuing vision of the white-robed chef bobbing up serenely at stated intervals and beginning a song that as frequently was forcibly checked amid his expostulations, until, at last, we three found ourselves in the moonlit village street outside the inn.

It must have been long past midnight, but instead of seeking our beds, as prudence — and our condition — dictated, we sought the seclusion of the forest. There, at the end of the long *allée*, chequered by light and shade, we came to a space more open, where the ground was silvered by the full flood of the high-riding moon. Here, in the middle of the road, we stretched ourselves at full length and discoursed — we could still talk — of many things of grave import, no doubt, though they escape my treacher-

Valima Feast

ous memory at the present time. How long we stayed there in this beatific state I know not, but finally Bob, rising to a sitting position, made the surprising statement that we were three idiots and might better be in bed. Somewhat pained, we nevertheless agreed with his concluding suggestion and, without too much difficulty, retraced our steps to our lodging.

Here I have a vision of Bob waving a bed-room candle from the stair leading to his room on the floor above that where Louis and I had ours, and sternly commanding me to see that his cousin got safely to bed. I took this command with a seriousness befitting the occasion, and at last, when Louis was properly robed for the night, I concluded my friendly service by carefully tucking in the covering. This I did in so conscientious a manner that my friend, smiling blandly from his pillow, murmured: "How good you are, you remind me of my mother." In after years, though I am forced to admit that the version of this story given by R. L. S. varied from my own truthful recital, we have often laughed over the baptism of Siron's grandchild, and his shade may now be smiling at me as I write.

Perhaps it may be well to explain here how little intemperance played a part in all our student gatherings. What little there was may be laid, I fear, at the door of the aliens; for among my French comrades it was virtually unknown. I can still see the extraordinary air of the connoisseur adopted by one of these last — by my friend Cocles, whose character I have described some pages back — when at the conclusion of a dinner he would consult the list of *vins fins*. "We will probably not order anything," he would gravely state, "but the very names of these wines have an aroma of their own." And then, lingering over the syllables, he would murmur, half to himself, the enchanting titles of the aristocratic offspring of the invigorating sun and the fruitful earth, concluding, perhaps, by ordering a modest half bottle of some well-known vintage, which, drop by drop, sharing with an appreciative friend, he would savour to the dregs.

With Stevenson, also, appreciation of the taste and the flavour of romance, which clings to the tradition of good wine, was as keen as his abhorrence of the intemperance that was common in Scotland. On the one hand, I remember his saying reflectively, over a final bottle of the Beaujolais-Fleury at Lavenues on the eve of one of his visits home, "I wish that we could get this in Edinburgh, for you don't know how I dread returning there and adapting myself to the ration of drink usual in the land of my fathers." On the other hand, I remember his exclamation, "Don't that make you just love France," when I told him the legend that there was a standing order in the French Army that no detachment of troops should ever pass the narrow strip of land on which ripens the noble *cru* of Clos Vougeot, without presenting arms.

Sins of omission and of commission were plentiful enough in my time among the students, as they had been probably since the first students sat on their tresses of straw and conversed in Latin in the rue de la Harpe, giving its name to the students' quarter, and as they are to-day within its enlarged boundaries; but over-indulgence in drink is not one of them, and it is as a somewhat extraordinary occurrence that I have ventured to tell this tale of "when the wine had done its rosy deed."

Robert Louis Stevenson

J. M. BARRIE

Some men of letters, not necessarily the greatest, have an indescribable charm to which we give our hearts. Thackeray is the young man's first love. Of living authors none perhaps bewitches the reader more than Mr Stevenson, who plays upon words as if they were a musical instrument. To follow the music is less difficult than to place the musician. A friend of mine, who, like Mr Grant Allen, reviews 365 books a year, and 366 in leap years, recently arranged the novelists of to-day in order of merit. Meredith, of course, he wrote first, and then there was a fall to Hardy. 'Haggard,' he explained, 'I dropped from the Eiffel Tower; but what can I do with Stevenson? I can't put him before Lorna Doone.' So Mr Stevenson puzzles the critics, fascinating them until they are willing to judge him by the great work he is to write by and by when the little books are finished. Over *Treasure Island* I let my fire die in winter without knowing that I was freezing. But the creator of Alan Breck has now published nearly twenty volumes. It is so much easier to finish the little works than to begin the great one, for which we are all taking notes.

Mr Stevenson is not to be labelled novelist. He wanders the byways of literature without any fixed address. Too much of a truant to be classified with the other boys, he is only a writer of fiction in the sense that he was once an Edinburgh University student because now and again he looked in at his classes when he happened to be that way. A literary man without a fixed occupation amazes Mr Henry James, a master in the school of fiction which tells, in three volumes, how Hiram K. Wilding trod on the skirt of Alice M. Sparkins without anything coming of it. Mr James analyses Mr Stevenson with immense cleverness, but without summing up. That *Dr Jekyll and Mr Hyde* should be by the author of *Treasure Island*, *Virginibus Puerisque* by the author of *The New Arabian Nights*, *A Child's Garden of Verses* by the author of *Prince Otto*, are to him the three degrees of comparison of wonder, though for my own part I marvel more that the author of *Daisy Miller*

should be Mr Stevenson's eulogist. One conceives Mr James a boy in velveteens looking fearfully at Stevenson playing at pirates.

There is nothing in Mr Stevenson's sometimes writing essays, sometimes romances, and anon poems to mark him versatile beyond other authors. One dreads his continuing to do so, with so many books at his back, lest it means weakness rather than strength. He experiments too long; he is still a boy wondering what he is going to be. With Cowley's candour he tells us that he wants to write something by which he may be for ever known. His attempts in this direction have been in the nature of trying different ways, and he always starts off whistling. Having gone so far without losing himself, he turns back to try another road. Does his heart fail him, despite his jaunty bearing, or is it because there is no hurry? Though all his books are obviously by the same hand, no living writer has come so near fame from so many different sides. Where is the man among us who could write another *Virginibus Puerisque*, the most delightful volume for the hammock ever sung in prose? The poems are as exquisite as they are artificial. *Jekyll and Hyde* is the greatest triumph extant in Christmas literature of the morbid kind. The donkey on the Cevennes (how Mr Stevenson belaboured him![1]) only stands second to the *Inland Voyage*. *Kidnapped* is the outstanding boy's book of its generation. *The Black Arrow* alone, to my thinking, is second class. We shall all be doleful if a marksman who can pepper his target with inners does not reach the bull's-eye. But it is quite time the great work was begun. The sun sinks while the climber walks round his mountain, looking for the best way up.

Hard necessity has kept some great writers from doing their best work, but Mr Stevenson is at last so firmly established that if he continues to be versatile it will only be from choice. He has attained a popularity such as is, as a rule, only accorded to classic authors or to charlatans. For this he has America to thank rather than Britain, for

---

[1] The donkey in question was of course female!

17 Heriot Row, Edinburgh

the Americans buy his books, the only honour a writer's admirers are slow to pay him. Mr Stevenson's reputation in the United States is creditable to that country, which has given him a position here in which only a few saw him when he left. Unfortunately, with popularity has come publicity. All day the reporters sit on his garden wall.

No man has written in a finer spirit of the profession of letters than Mr Stevenson, but this gossip vulgarises it. The adulation of the American public and of a little band of clever literary dandies in London, great in criticism, of whom he had become the darling, has made Mr Stevenson complacent, and he always tended perhaps to be a thought too fond of his velvet coat. There is danger in the delight with which his every scrap is now received. A few years ago, when he was his own severest and sanest critic, he stopped the publication of a book after it was in proof — a brave act. He has lost this courage, or he would have re-writtten *The Black Arrow*. There is deterioration in the essays he has been contributing to an American magazine, graceful and suggestive though they are. The most charming of living stylists, Mr Stevenson is self-conscious in all his books now and again, but hitherto it has been the self-consciousness of an artist with severe critics at his shoulder. It has become self-satisfaction. The critics have put a giant's robe on him, and he has not flung it off. He dismisses *Tom Jones* with a simper. Personally Thackeray 'scarce appeals to us as the ideal gentleman; if there were nothing else [what else is there?], perpetual nosing after snobbery at least suggests the snob.' From Mr Stevenson one would not have expected the revival of this silly charge, which makes a cabbage of every man who writes about cabbages. I shall say no more of these ill-considered papers, though the sneers at Fielding call for indignant remonstrance, beyond expressing a hope that they lie buried between magazine covers. Mr Stevenson has reached the critical point in his career, and one would like to see him back at Bournemouth, writing within high walls. We want that big book; we think he is capable of it, and so we cannot afford to let him drift into the seaweed. About the writer with whom his name is so often absurdly linked we feel differently. It is as foolish to rail at Mr Rider Haggard's complacency as it would be to blame Christopher Sly for so quickly believing that he was born a lord.

Swanston Cottage

The keynote of all Mr Stevenson's writings is his indifference, so far as his books are concerned, to the affairs of life and death on which other minds are chiefly set. Whether man has an immortal soul interests him as an artist not a whit: what is to come of man troubles him as little as where man came from. He is a warm, genial writer, yet this is so strange as to seem inhuman. His philosophy is that we are but as the light-hearted birds. This is our moment of being; let us play the intoxicating game of life beautifully, artistically, before we fall dead from the tree. We all know it is only in his books that Mr Stevenson can live this life. The cry is to arms; spears glisten in the sun; see the brave bark riding joyously on the waves, the black flag, the dash of red colour twisting round a mountainside. Alas! the drummer lies on a couch beating his drum. It is a pathetic picture, less true to fact now, one rejoices to know, than it was recently. A common theory is that Mr Stevenson dreams an ideal life to escape from his own sufferings. This sentimental plea suits very well. The noticeable thing, however, is that the grotesque, the uncanny, holds his soul; his brain will only follow a coloured clue. The result is that he is chiefly picturesque, and, to those who want more than art for art's sake, never satisfying. Fascinating as his verses are, artless in the perfection of art, they take no reader a step forward. The children of whom he sings so sweetly are

Valima: interior

cherubs without souls. It is not in poetry that Mr Stevenson will give the great book to the world, nor will it, I think, be in the form of essays. Of late he has done nothing quite so fine as *Virginibus Puerisque*, though most of his essays are gardens in which grow few weeds. Quaint in matter as in treatment, they are the best strictly literary essays of the day, and their mixture of tenderness with humour suggests Charles Lamb. Some think Mr Stevenson's essays equal to Lamb's, or greater. To that I say No. The name of Lamb will for many a year bring proud tears to English eyes. Here was a man, weak like the rest of us, who kept his sorrows to himself. Life to him was not among the trees. He had loved and lost. Grief laid a heavy hand on his brave brow. Dark were his nights;

horrid shadows in the house; sudden terrors; the heart stops beating waiting for a footstep. At that door comes Tragedy, knocking at all hours. Was Lamb dismayed? The tragedy of his life was not drear to him. It was wound round those who were dearest to him; it let him know that life has a glory even at its saddest, that humour and pathos clasp hands, that loved ones are drawn nearer, and the soul strengthened in the presence of anguish, pain, and death. When Lamb sat down to write he did not pull down his blind on all that is greatest, if most awful, in human life. He was gentle, kindly; but he did not play at pretending that there is no cemetery round the corner. In Mr Stevenson's exquisite essays one looks in vain for the great heart that palpitates through the pages of Charles Lamb.

The great work, if we are not to be disappointed, will be fiction. Mr Stevenson is said to feel this himself, and, as I understand, *Harry Shovel* will be his biggest bid for fame. It is to be, broadly speaking, a nineteenth-century *Peregrine Pickle*, dashed with Meredith, and this in the teeth of many admirers who maintain that the best of the author is Scottish. Mr Stevenson, however, knows what he is about. Critics have said enthusiastically — for it is difficult to write of Mr Stevenson without enthusiasm — that Alan Breck is as good as anything in Scott. Alan Breck is certainly a masterpiece, quite worthy of the greatest of all storytellers, who, nevertheless, it should be remembered, created these rich side characters by the score, another before dinner-time. English critics have taken Alan to their hearts, and appreciate him thoroughly; the reason, no doubt, being that he is the character whom England acknowledges as the Scottish type. The Highlands, which are Scotland to the same extent as Northumberland is England, present such a character to this day, but no deep knowledge of Mr Stevenson's native country was required to reproduce him. An artistic Englishman or American could have done it. Scottish religion, I think, Mr Stevenson has never understood, except as the outsider misunderstands it. He thinks it hard because there are no coloured windows. 'The colour of Scotland has entered into him altogether,' says Mr James, who, we gather, conceives in Edinburgh Castle a place where tartans glisten in the sun, while rocks re-echo bagpipes. Mr James is right in a way. It is the tartan, the claymore, the cry that the heather is on fire, that are Scotland to Mr Stevenson. But the Scotland of our day is not a country rich in colour; a sombre grey prevails. Thus, though Mr Stevenson's best romance is Scottish, that is only, I think, because of his extraordinary aptitude for the picturesque. Give him any period in any country that is romantic, and he will soon steep himself in the kind of knowledge he can best turn to account. Adventures suit him best, the ladies being left behind; and so long as he is in fettle it matters little whether the scene be Scotland or Spain. The great thing is that he should now give to one ambitious book the time in which he has hitherto written half a dozen small ones. He will have to take existence a little more seriously — to weave broadcloth instead of lace.

"R. L. S."

W. E. HENLEY

Mr Graham Balfour has done his best; and his best should rank decently among official biographies. He is loving, he is discreet, he has much knowledge. Indeed, almost the worst that can be said of him is that he is a day or so after the fair. We live so fast, and our reading is so many weeks ahead of death and time, that the moment for the official biography of Robert Lewis Stevenson seems already one with dead Yesterday, if not the day before that. That is as may be. As to Mr Balfour's tact and piety (a most serviceable blend), there cannot be two opinions: he has written lovingly of his dead cousin, and, according to his lights, he has written well. I mean, he has done his best for the Stevenson of legend and his best for the Stevenson of life. So far as I can see, he does not distinguish the one from the other: his predilections are all with rumour and report; and if they be not, at least he can govern his tongue. On the whole, I may congratulate him on his result.

Yet I confess that "it do not overstimulate." I cannot lay a finger on any point in this biography, excepting here and there whereat I have a peculiar interest, and say that Mr Balfour has not done his utmost, and is not, as an official biographer, entirely successful. Yet am I discontented, dissatisfied, still looking for more. I daresay the feeling is personal; that I cannot judge equably, for I know too much. So be it. 'Tis a fact that, recalling what I can recall, I can only take Mr Balfour's book as a solemn and serious essay in that kind of make-believe in which the biographee (if one may use so flippant a neologism in so august a connexion) did all his life rejoice, and was exceeding glad. I read; and as I read I am oppressed by the thought that here is Lewis Stevenson very much as he may well have wanted to be, but that here is not Lewis Stevenson at all. At any rate, here is not the Lewis Stevenson I knew. At this place let me take refuge in an analogy. Mr Balfour's first volume is prefaced by a portrait. It is not unlike in certain ways, yet it set me wondering how and when and by whom that brilliant face

Letter from R.L.S. to W.E. Henley

had been thus commonly transfigured. I looked for information, and then I saw why this very feminine view of a very masculine creature had got itself such currency as print can give. I do not want to make Mr Graham Balfour blush for his loyalty; but I can't help the reflection that, even as the portrait is smooth, and smiling, and ladylike, and unexceptionable, so, in less degree, is his *Life*. What astonishes me, what commands my admiration, is that he has done so well that even I can read him with interest, and can recommend him to all them that would still be sentimentalising about R. L. S.

For me there were two Stevensons: the Stevenson who went to America in '87; and the Stevenson who never came back. The first I knew, and loved; the other I lost touch with, and, though I admired him, did not greatly esteem. My relation to him was that of a man with a grievance; and for that reason, perhaps — that reason and others — I am by no means disposed to take all Mr Balfour says for gospel, nor willing to forget, on the showing of what is after all an official statement, the knowledge gained in an absolute intimacy of give-and-take which lasted for thirteen years, and includes so many of the circumstances of those thirteen years that, as I believe, none living now can pretend to speak of them with any such authority as mine. This, however, is not to say that Mr Balfour's view of his famous cousin is not warranted to the letter, so far as he saw and knew. I mean no more than that the Stevenson he knew was not the Stevenson who came to me (that good angel, Mr Leslie Stephen, aiding) in the old Edinburgh Infirmary; nor the Stevenson I nursed in secret, hard by the old Bristo Port, till he could make shift to paddle the *Arethusa*; nor the Stevenson who stayed with me at Acton after selling Modestine, nor even the Stevenson who booked a steerage berth to New York and thence trained it "across the plains," and ended for the time being as a married man and a Silverado squatter; though I confess that in this last avatar the Stevenson of Mr Balfour's dream had begun, however faintly and vaguely, to adumbrate himself, and might have been looked for as a certainty by persons less affectionate and uninquiring than those by whom he was then approached. Mr Balfour does me the honour of quoting the sonnet into which I crammed my impressions of my companion and friend; and, since he has done so, I may as well own that "the Shorter Catechist" of the last verse was an afterthought. In those days he was in abeyance, to say the least; and if, even then, *il allait poindre à l'horizon* (as the composition, in secret and as if ashamed, of *Lay Morals* persuades me to believe he did), I, at any rate, was too short-sighted to suspect his whereabouts. When I realised it, I completed my sonnet; but this was not till years had come and gone, and the Shorter Catechist, already detested by more than one, was fully revealed to me.

I will say at once that I do not love the Shorter Catechist, in anybody, and that I loved him less in Stevenson than anywhere that I have ever found him. He is too selfish and too self-righteous a beast for me. He makes ideals for himself with a resolute regard for his own salvation; but he is all-too apt to damn the rest of the world for declining to live up to them, and he is all-too ready to make a lapse of his own the occasion for a rule of conduct for himself and the lasting pretext for a highly moral deliverance to such backsliding Erastians as, having memories and a certain concern for facts, would like him to wear his rue with a difference. At bottom Stevenson was an excellent fellow. But he was of his essence what the French call *personnel*. He was, that is, incessantly and passionately interested in Stevenson. He could not be in the same room with a mirror but he must invite its confidences every time he passed it; to him there was nothing obvious in time and eternity, and the smallest of his discoveries, his most trivial apprehensions, were all by way of being revelations, and as revelations must be thrust upon the world; he was never so much in earnest, never so well pleased (this were he happy or wretched), never so irresistible, as when he wrote about himself. Withal, if he wanted a thing, he went after it with an entire contempt for consequences. For these, indeed, the Shorter Catechist was ever prepared to answer; so that, whether he did well or ill, he was safe to come out unabashed and cheerful. He detested Mr Gladstone, I am pleased to say; but his gift of self-persuasion was scarce second to that statesman's own. He gave himself out for the most openminded of men: to him one point of view was as good as another; Age's was respectable, but so was Youth's; the Fox that had a tail was no whit more considerable than the Fox whose tail was lost. *Et patati, et patata.* 'Twas all "as easy as lying" to him, for 'twas all in the run of his humanity. But in the event it was academic; for where he was grossly interested, he could see but one side of the debate; and there are people yet living (I am not one of them) who, knowing him intimately, have not hestitated to describe him in a word of three letters, the suspicion of which might well make him turn in his grave. And yet, I do not know. He ever took himself so seriously — or rather

Valima: House and Vaea mountain

he ever played at life with such a solemn grace — that perhaps, after all, he would scarce stir where he lies for the dread vocable. For he was a humourist and a thinker, and could he hear it, he would certainly smile, fall (like the Faquir of story) to considering himself umbilically, and, finding in the end that he had fairly earned it, go back to sleep, with a glow of satisfaction for that this part also had been well played. No better histrion ever lived. But in the South Seas the mask got set, the "lines" became a little stereotyped. Plainly the Shorter Catechist was what was wanted. And here we are: with Stevenson's later letters and Mr Graham Balfour's estimate.

'Tis as that of an angel clean from heaven, and I for my part flatly refuse to recognise it. Not, if I can help it, shall this faultless, or very nearly faultless, monster go down to after years as the Lewis I knew, and loved, and laboured with and for, with all my heart and strength and understanding. In days to come I may write as much as can be told of him. Till those days come, this protest must suffice. If it convey the impression that I take a view of Stevenson which is my own, and which declines to be concerned with this Seraph in chocolate, this barley-sugar effigy of a real man; that the best and the most interesting part of Stevenson's life will never get written — even by me; and that the Shorter Catechist of Vailima, however brilliant and distingushed as a writer of stories, however authorised and acceptable as an artist in morals, is not my old, riotous, intrepid, scornful Stevenson at all — suffice it will.

For the rest, I think he has written himself down in terms that may not be mistaken, nor improved, in a fragment of an essay on morals printed in the *Appendix* to the *Edinburgh Edition.* "An unconscious, easy, selfish person," he remarks, "shocks less, and is more easily loved, than one who is laboriously and egotistically unselfish. There is at least no fuss about the first; but the other parades his sacrifices, and so sells his favours too dear. Selfishness is calm, a force of nature: you might say the trees are selfish. But egoism is a piece of vanity; it must always take you into its confidence; it is uneasy, troublesome, searching; it can do good, but not hand-somely; it is uglier, because less dignified than selfish itself. But here," he goes on, with that careful candour which he so often has, "here I perhaps exaggerate to myself, because I am the one more then the other, and feel it like a hook in my mouth at every step I take. *Do what I will, this seems to spoil all.*" This, as it seems to me, describes him so exactly that, if you allow for histrionics (no inconsiderable thing, remember!), you need no more description. It was said of him, once, that when he wrote of anything, he wrote it with such an implacable lucidity as left it beggared of mystery. This is what he has done in this passage; and who runs may read him in it as he was. 'Tis to this anxious and uncloistered egotism of his that we are indebted for so much good writing in the matter of confession and self-revelation. To this the circumstance is due that when the Amateur Emigrant asked his friend, the Blacksmith, how — speaking as man to man; as one in the

steerage to another — he had behaved on the voyage, he was staggered by the reply that he had done not so badly "on the whole." 'Tis to this that we are indebted for the prayers, the supplications for valour, the vocalisings about duty (which the most of us do as a matter of course), by which that part of the world which reads Stevenson — (and that part of it which does not is happily the smaller) — has long been, and is still being, joyously edified.

Mr Balfour notes with tender admiration that, when Stevenson had quarrelled with anybody, he was always trying to do that person a service in secret. But if this be not the hero of my quotation all over: salving his conscience for a possble injustice, done in heat and apprehended too late for anything but a frank avowal and a complete apology; which, in the circumstances, the Shorter Catechist finds abhorrent, and therefore immor-al: then self-analysis is of no moment, and confession means nothing, and no virtue is left in words. And in the manner of his giving, as exampled by Mr Balfour, the Anxious Egotist is characteristically and not pleasantly apparent. "I hereby authorise you," he writes, "to pay when necessary £——— to Z———: if I gave him more, it would only lead to his starting a gig and keeping a Pomeranian dog." 'Tis wittily put, of course; but it scarce becomes the lips of a man who had several kennels of Pomeranians, kept gigs innumerable, reported that brilliant and taking little talk between Count Spada and the General of the Jesuits, realised the place in God's economy of "The singer on the garden seat," and held as an essential gospel that an act may be forgiven of the Deities, but that to neglect an opportunity, to hang back, to do nothing when something might be done — this, this is the Unpardonable Sin. Alas! there be special sorts of gigs, and who shall number the varieties of the Pomera-nian dog? And from my heart I wish that Mr Balfour had left that utterance of one who bred Pomeranians and kept gigs — sometimes, it may be, with a moral aim, but always as seemed good to him — unguessed and unreported. But to your Anxious Egotist, your trained and cultured Shorter Catechist, what magnificence in the matter of self-approval, self-oblivion, self-righteousness could come amiss? Stevenson's world was ever "a brave gymnasium," more or less; but if there were room in it for "the singer on the garden seat," it was only as a romanic object. He had no real part in this philosopher's economy of things, since he might dare nothing at this philosopher's cost. In a "brave gymnasium" ordered on these lines the gigs and the Pomeranians all went one way; and that, despite all Stevenson's protestings, was not the way of Stevenson's *bénéficiaires*. 'Tis the oddest of revelations; but 'tis of Mr Balfour's making, not Stevenson's. He, I am sure, would cheerfully have gone to the stake, like the good and constant histrion he was, or ever he would have given it to the world in what he used to call "cold, hard print."

But I must call a truce, and leave cavilling. I long to say that 'tis wonderful to me, who have forgot so much, to find so much of myself in Stevenson and in Stevenson's biographer. I take up a volume of the *Edinburgh Edition*, and I read that, included in the plenishing of his ideal house, are "a Canaletto print or two"; and I recall the circumstance that his taste for Canaletto prints, even as his Canaletto prints themselves, came through and from me. I bought them, I remember, in the Knightsbridge Road, and he paid me what I gave for them, which was some six or seven shillings apiece. I turn the page, and read of "Piranesi etchings on the walls"; and I remember who placed them there, and the blessed hours I've had in their neighbourhood. I turn the page again, and I come on the *Moral Emblems* and *Not I*; and once more the Muse of Memory is too much for me, and, as in a dream I see myself touting in the interest of these works, taking sixpence of this one and eightpence of that other, and embezzling these receipts: for I neither paid the laborious graver-poet the price of his endeavour, nor delivered the works for which I was acting as agent. But, returning to Mr Balfour's book, I open it at random; I read that "Bob Stevenson came, and I can never be grateful enough for what he did for me then"; and the Muse once more awakens me. I recall the despairing telegram which reached me late one night; the call on my good friend, the late Constantine Ionides, for ready money; the journey through Westbourne Grove (the blazing central telegraph office by the way) to St. John's Wood, where Bob and his wife resided. I think it was in Acacia Road. But I know that I blundered: that I went to the wrong house, and, by appealing to a bell disturbed a lady (whom I imagine to have been but parcel-dressed) in the practice of her avocations. Over a garden-wall, and with a garden-door between, I explained the nature of my errand to her; was dismissed in terms whose frostiness still hangs glittering about my remembrance; groped my way till I found the house I wanted; and, after knocking and ringing till my heart went into my stomach, and Lewis's death in a foreign land was merely a matter of hours to me, roused Bob from his bed, intimated my views, and produced "the wherewithal." His eyes were heavy with sleep, but he started next day. Or it is a casual mention of "Z———": a very casual mention. And again the Muse appeals to me, and recalls how "Z———" chucked his practice and went to Hyères at a dozen hours' notice, did his best — (I wish I could write what it was) — and suddenly became a person in the Stevensonian Hierarchy; but presently, saying or doing something somebody or other did not like, was disseated, cast into outer darkness, and not so much as named — (such is the Anxious Egotist!) — among the innumerable doctors who figure, with Dr Scott, of Bournemouth, at the head of them, in the dedication of one of Stevenson's books. With what an instancy the circumstances of what dispatch — the how, the when, the whence — leap to my pen's end as I write! For the moment I forget myself; and 'tis something of an effort to recall that Stevenson is dead, but "Z———" is yet in complete and cheerful activity, recking naught of his exclusion from Stevenson's list, and doing his best for low and high, as he was doing it when he came into my life some and twenty years ago.

A sentence in the Dedication (suppressed; but finally printed in the *Edinburgh Edition*) of *The Master of Ballantrae*, reminds me of a certain *Ballade Stevenson*, for which I am responsible, and which I preferred (and so, I think, did he), above the sonnet. "I would have all literature bald," so the sentence goes, "*and all authors (if you like) but one.*" That brings back my ballade, with its refrain, "A bald and cullid-headed man"; and that refrain in its turn brings back the days of what the two Stevensons, Bob and Lewis, knew as "jink". The beginning is a sentence in Artemus Ward. It runs (I must quote from memory) thus:— "'Twas the lone sunset hour. Three bald-headed cullid men was playing monte; all was peas;" and it so took hold upon the two Stevensons that, first of all, "bald-headed and cullid," and then, by a natural transition, "bald and

Stevenson and family, Sydney

cullid-headed" became their favourite description of any and everything preferred by them — a passage in Shakespeare, an achievement in whisky and sheep's head, a good talk, a notable drunk, a fair woman. This I remembered, and hence my refrain. How I wish I could recall those three octaves and that envoy! Why did Mr

Balfour not resuscitate this dead and forgotten masterpiece? 'Tis as good of its kind as any of my nicknames for him: Fastidious Brisk and (especially) the *in*delicate Ariel. Another nickname, by the way, which Mr Balfour does not quote, came from the Parliament House. "Here," quoth the jolly creature who invented it (he was afterwards, and perhaps still is, a sheriff-substitute somewhere or other) — "Here comes the Gifted Boy." Thus, and not otherwise, Peter Robertson took on, as they say, "Peveril of the Peak" and was instantly retorted upon as "Peter of the Painch." In Stevenson's case there was no response. The nickname troubled him for a moment; but he had nothing to say to it. In truth, he loved not to be thus attacked, and was in such cases sometimes at a loss for words. He shone in debate, and he excelled in talk. But in both talk and debate he was strung to his highest pitch — alert, daring, of an inextinguishable gaiety, quick and resourceful to the nth degree; and try to fall with him then was to get badly handled, if not utterly suppressed. But he was not averse from monologue — far from it; and I have sometimes thought that he ran his temperament too hard. Also, was he what the world calls "a wit"? I do not think he was. After all, a wit is a man of phrases: consciously, sometimes, he waits, he thinks, he condenses his thought, and out comes his witticism; or he waits not, nor thinks, nor condenses, but says something, and by no sort of effort he retorts in the only possible way. Mr Thackeray has noted the difference between old Mr Congreve, inventing his epigrams in a corner, and young Mr Harry Fielding, who pours out everything he has in his heart, and is, in effect, as brilliant, as engaging, and as arresting a talker as Colonel Esmond has known. In print Stevenson was now and then witty enough for seven; but in talk his way was, not Congreve's but, Harry Fielding's. No; he was certainly not a wit, in the sense that Congreve was a wit. Perhaps he was nearer than he knew to that Jack Fletcher — (he talked comedies, his printer says) — for whom, having begun his later life, and being somewhat stricken with respectability, he could find no better description to me than "a dirty dog"; perhaps (of the Samoan Stevenson I will say at once that I do not for one moment think so) he would have relished Fielding, and found himself, so to speak, in that most gallant, cheerful pratical-artist soul. But Fielding and Fletcher certainly, and Congreve probably, would have had a retort, or courteous or the other thing, for the author of that rather marking phrase — The Gifted Boy." And Stevenson, who was not a wit, but something a thousand times better, had none. No "Peter of the Painch" occurred to this new Peveril of the Peak; and that was Lewis's way. Give him all that Mrs

Battle asked, and he was almost inimitable. Come to him suddenly: "prop him on the nose," as it were: and he was tame. And so much now for that far-glancing, variously coloured, intensely romantic and flagrantly humorous expression of life — the talk of R. L. S.

Follow the Henley-Stevenson plays. But how to deal with them? Mr Balfour gives us a list of those projected and those done; and having forgotten all about it, I find that list most interesting. It reads well, even now; for I fear that one of our first cares was to find a good name for the still unattempted piece; and Mr Balfour's quotation, if it show nothing else, will show that in this endeavour we were not wholly unsuccessful. *Honour and Arms* — is not a canorous and inspiriting title? And *The King of Clubs* — reader, does that promise nothing? And *The Tragedy of Hester Noble* — how is that for a play bill? *Ajax* I pass, though (coming after Sophocles) we never made so good a play. But *Farmer George* (of which I remember nothing whatever) at any rate sounds well. Comes *The Mother-in-Law*; and that would have been a tragedy. As to *Madame Fate* and *Madame Destiny*, I cannot recall a single particular; but I *do* remember that the first touch was mine, and that the second title is merely an improvement on the first. To go back a little: *Honour and Arms* is of its essence English, Jacobitish, romantic; the hero is sorely tried; love is too much for duty; and if I remember aright, he emerges ill from his trial. But his father (Sir Austin Fielding), is a noble old boy; his mistress (Jean Lorimer: Jean — or is it Barbara?) is a noble young girl. And when I tell you that William of Orange is the *deus ex machinâ*; that Harry Fielding was broke and sentenced to be shot; that Sir Austin pleaded with the King, with Ginkel, and the Scots soldier of fortune who had witnessed Harry's failure; that then the Lorimers came in, and the *scène-à-faire* was (in our strong conceit) as good as done; so that Harry took back his sword and married his Barbara (or his Jean), and Sir Austin (he was really Tom Stevenson) played the Scottish Father, and even Dutch William was moved to a genial saying — reader mine, if I tell you that much, won't you be sorry, sorry while life is in you, that you will never see that play? And may I, if you aren't — may I, with or without offence, at once assert that you know nothing about plays? Well, well . . . in those days, as Mr Balfour very justly puts it, we — I and

Lewis — knew nothing neither. All the same, it was a golden time. I stole the idea of *The King of Clubs* from *The Old Curiosity Shop*, and found more to thieve years afterwards in *Old St. Paul's*; it was invented for that excellent actor, Mr. Shiel Barry; a chief character was called the Hon. Aquila Breckenridge (if anything could be more American than that name, I'd like to see it); the scene was New Orleans somewhere about 1830. It was all so taking and extreme, and Barry was so exactly what we wanted, that I wonder now that it never got written. That it and the rest were left in the shape of Good Intentions, to crawl the floor of hell with the good Bishop's span-long babes, was owing, I think, to the fact that both collaborators wanted money, and had got sick and tired of the Abstract Actor. Had we been men of substance — men able to take a theatre and pay their players to do as they were told — we might possibly have persisted, and done what was in us to re-create the Romantic Drama in the terms of prose. But we were not men of substance; and our consideration of the Abstract Actor very soon convinced us that, if he had anything to do with it, men of substance we should never be. "Et voilà pourquoi votre fille est muette": that is why the Muse of Romantic Drama, the Muse of *Anthony* and *Carmosine*, of *On ne badine pas avec l'amour* and *la Tour de Nesle*, stands where and as she did, before we scrimmaged for her favours.

Lewis the musician, too — how much I saw of him! how often have I ministered to his artless and homely needs! Like his cousin, Stevenson, had no ear for intervals: his one tune for many years was *Auld Lang Syne*, which he sang, in the belief that it was a genuine Scots melody, to all manner of verses, decent sometimes, improvised or recalled as occasion or inspiration served. Yet had he an aery and delicate sense of rhythm; and I have ever regretted that he did not study music from the first. Not, of course, for creation's sake; for at the best he could never have been anything but what his cousin used to call a Mus. Doc. — a plodder equally uninspired, uninterest- ing, and superfluous: not, I say, for music's sake, but for that of his own vigilant, enquiring, far-wondering, extremely technical mind, which might often and for long spaces of time have found in Bach and Beethoven, or even in Purcell and Lulli and Couperin, the refreshment it had to seek, and did, in Xavier de Montépin and Fortuné du Boisgobey. I, for my part, know nothing of the mathema- tics of music; but in those days I strummed the piano a little, and I was, as they say, "no mean performer" on the tin whistle:—

> "Once again,
> O thou, Orpheus andd Herakles, the Bard
> And the Deliverer, touch the stops again":—

so that it fell to me to teach him the difference between *The Mill, Mill, O* and (say) *Fra Poco*, both of which come very fairly well on the humbler instrument, and on the other to shadow forth some vague yet painful hints of the enormous and distressing suggestiveness which Beeth- oven expressed into the slow movements of his sonatas. Gluck, too, was a household word with us; so were Handel and Mozart; and as for jigs and reels ——! Well, well; it's all over now, and I've made no attempt at making music since seven years. But we are told that the mathematics of music, as they appeared to Stevenson's imagination, whether technical or creative, were at once a solace to him, and a great distraction; and I love to think that I helped him, insistently helped him, to venture outside his art, and to carve out for his mind this tiny brigand-state in an immense enchanted kingdom, where, had he not been himself, he had no business at all to be.

I have said nothing of Stevenson the artist in this garrulous and egotistic pronouncement of his official *Life*; for the very simple reason that I have nothing to say. To tell the truth, his books are none of mine: I mean, that if I want reading, I do not go for it to the *Edinburgh Edition*. I am not interested in remarks about morals; in and out of letters I have lived a full and varied life, and my opinions are my own. So, if I crave the enchantment of romance, I ask it of bigger men than he, and of bigger books than his: of *Esmond* (say) and *Great Expectations*, of *Redgauntlet* and *Old Mortality*, of *la Reine Margot* and *Bragelonne*, of *David Copperfield* and *A Tale of Two Cities*: while, if good writing and some other things be in my appetite, are there not always Hazlitt and Lamb — to say nothing of that "globe of miraculous continents" which is known to us as Shakespeare? There is his style, you will say; and it is a fact that it is rare, and in the last times better, because much simpler, than in the first. But after all, his style is so perfectly achieved that the achievement gets obvious: and

R.L.S. after his father's death

when achievement gets obvious, is it not by way of becoming uninteresting? And is there not something to be said for the person who wrote that Stevenson always reminded him of a young man dressed the best he ever saw for the Burlington Arcade? Stevenson's work in letters does not now take me much, and I decline to enter on the question of its immortality; since that, despite what any can say, will get itself settled, soon or late, for all time. No; when I care to think of Stevenson it is not of "R. L. S.": R. L. S. "the renowned, the accomplished, Executing his difficult solo:" but of the "Lewis" that I knew, and loved, and wrought for, and worked with for so long. The successful man of letters does not greatly interest me: I read his careful prayers, and pass on, with the certainty that, well as they read, they were not written for print; I learn of his nameless prodigalities — and recall some instances of conduct in another vein. I remember, rather, the unmarried and irresponsible Lewis: the friend, the comrade, the *charmeur*. Truly, that last word, French as it is, is the only one that is worthy of him. I shall ever remember him as that. The impression of his writings disappears; the impression of himself and his talk is ever a possession. He had, as I have said elsewhere, all the gifts (he and his cousin, he and Bob) that qualify the talker's temperament:— "As voice and eye and laugh, look and gesture, humour and fantasy, audacity and agility of mind, a lively and most impudent invention, a copious vocabulary, a right gift of foollery, a just inevitable sense of right and wrong" (this though I've blamed him for a tendency to monologue, and a trick of depending too much on his temperament). And I take leave to repeat what I've said elsewhere, that those who know him only by his books — (I think our Fleeming Jenkin, were he alive, would back me here) — know but the poorest of him. Forasmuch as he was primarily a talker, his printed works, like those of others after his kind, are but a sop for posterity:— "A last dying speech and confession (as it were) to show that not for nothing were they held rare fellows in their day."

A last word. I have everywhere read that we must praise him now and always for that, being a stricken man, he would live out his life. Are we not all stricken men, and do we not all do that? And why, because he wrote better than any one, should he have praise and fame for doing that which many a poor, consumptive sempstress does: cheerfully, faithfully, with no eloquent appeals to God, nor so much as a paragraph in the evening papers? That a man writes well at death's door is sure no reason for making him a hero; for, after all, there is as much virtue in making a shirt, or finishing a gross of match-boxes, in the very act of mortality, as there is in polishing a verse, or completing a chapter in a novel. As much, I say; but is there not an immense deal more? In the one case, the sufferer does the thing he loves best in life. In the other, well — who that has not made shirts, or finished match-boxes, shall speak? Stevenson, for all his vocalisings, was a brave man, with a fine, buoyant spirit; and he took the mystery of life and time and death as seemed best to him. But we are mortals all; and, so far as I have seen there are few of us but strive to keep a decent face for the Arch-Discomforter. There is no wonder that Stevenson wrote his best in the shadow of the Shade; for writing his best was very life to him. Why, then, all this crawling astonishment — this voluble admiration? If it meant anything, it would mean that we have forgotten how to live, and that none of us is prepared to die; and that were an outrage on the innumerable unstoried martyrdoms of humanity. Let this be said of him, once for all: "He was a good man, good at many things, and now this also he has attained to, to be at rest." That covers Sophocles and Shakespeare, Marlborough and Bonaparte. Let it serve for Stevenson; and, for ourselves, let us live and die uninsulted, as we lived and died before his books began to sell and his personality was a marketable thing.

Robert Louis Stevenson

HENRY JAMES

It was the happy fortune of Robert Louis Stevenson to have created beyond any man of his craft in our day a body of readers inspired with the feelings that we for the most part place at the service only of those for whom our affection is personal. There was no one who knew the man, one may safely assert, who was not also devoted to the writer — conforming in this respect to a general law (if law it be) that shows us many exceptions; but, naturally and not inconveniently, it had to remain far from true that all devotees of the writer were able to approach the man. The case was nevertheless that the man somehow approached *them*, and that to read him — certainly to read him with the full sense of his charm — came to mean for many persons much the same as to "meet" him. It was as if he wrote himself outright and altogether, rose straight to the surface of his prose, and still more of his happiest verse; so that these things gave out, besides whatever else, his look and motions and voice, showed his life and manners, all that there was of him, his "tremendous secrets" not excepted. We grew in short to possess him entire, and the example is the more curious and beautiful as he neither made a business of "confession" nor cultivated most those forms through which the *ego* shines. His great successes were supposititious histories of persons quite different from himself, and the objective, as we learned to call it, was the ideal to which he oftenest sacrificed.

The effect of it all none the less was such that his Correspondence has only seemed to administer delightfully a further push to a door already half open and through which we enter with an extraordinary failure of any sense of intrusion. We feel indeed that we are living with him, but what is that but what we were doing before? Through his Correspondence certainly the *ego* does, magnificently, shine — which is much the best thing that in any correspondence it can ever do. But even the "Vailima Letters," published by Mr Sidney Colvin in 1895, had already both established that and allayed our diffidence. "It came over me the other day suddenly that this diary of mine to you would make good pickings after I am dead, and a man could make some kind of book out of it without much trouble. So, for God's sake, don't lose them."

Being on these terms with our author, and feeling as if we had always been, we profit by freedoms that seem but the consecration of intimacy. Not only have we no sense of intrusion, but we are so prepared to penetrate further than when we come to limits we quite feel as if the story were mutilated and the copy not complete. There it is precisely that we seize the secret of our tie. Of course it was personal, for how did it operate in any connection whatever but to make us live with him? We had lived with him in "Treasure Island," in "Kidnapped" and in "Catriona," just as we do, by the light of these posthumous volumes, in the South Seas and at Vailima; and our present confidence comes from the fact of a particularly charming continuity. It is not that his novels were "subjective", but that his life was romantic, and in the very same degree in which his own conception, his own presentation, of that element touches and thrills. If we want to know even more it is because we are always and everywhere in the story.

To this absorbing extension of the story then the two volumes of Letters[1] now published by Mr Sidney Colvin beautifully contribute. The shelf of our library that contains our best letterwriters is considerably furnished, but not overcrowded, and its glory is not too great to keep Stevenson from finding there a place with the very first. He will not figure among the writers — those apt in this line to enjoy precedence — to whom only small things happen and who beguile us by making the most of them; he belongs to the class who have both matter and manner, substance and spirit, whom life carries swiftly before it

[1] "The Letters of Robert Louis Stevenson to his Family and Friends Selected and Edited, with Notes and Introduction, by Sidney Colvin." 1899.

and who signal and communicate, not to say gesticulate, as they go. He lived to the topmost pulse, and the last thing that could happen was that he should find himself on any occasion with nothing to report. Of all that he may have uttered on certain occasions we are inevitably not here possessed — a fact that, as I have hinted above, affects us, perversely, as an inexcusable gap in the story; but he never fails of the thing that we most love letters for, the full expression of the moment and the mood, the actual good or bad or middling, the thing in his head, his heart or his house. Mr Colvin has given us an admirable "Introduction" — a characterisation of his friend so founded at once on knowledge and on judgment that the whole sense of the man strikes us as extracted in it. He has elucidated each group or period with notes that leave nothing to be desired; and nothing remains that I can think of to thank him for unless the intimation that we may yet look for another volume — which, however much more free it might make us of the author's mystery, we should accept, I repeat, with the same absence of scruple. Nothing more belongs to our day than this question of the inviolable, of the rights of privacy and the justice of our claim to aid from editors and other retailers in getting behind certain eminent or defiant appearances; and the general knot so presented is indeed a hard one to untie. Yet we may take it for a matter regarding which such publications as Mr Colvin's have much to suggest.

There is no absolute privacy — save of course when the exposed subject may have wished or endeavoured positively to constitute it; and things too sacred are often only things that are not perhaps at all otherwise superlative. One may hold both that people — that artists perhaps in particular — are well advised to cover their tracks, and yet that our having gone behind, or merely stayed before, in a particular case, may be a minor question compared with our having picked up a value. Personal records of the type before us can at any rate obviously be but the reverse of a deterrent to the urged inquirer. They are too happy an instance — they positively make for the risked indiscretion. Stevenson never covered his tracks, and the tracks prove perhaps to be what most attaches us. We follow them here, from year to year and from stage to stage, with the same charmed sense with which he has made us follow some hunted hero

Rob and Ben

or

The P I R A T E and the A P O T H E C A R Y .

Scene the Third.

From the script of *The Pirate and the Apothecary*

in the heather. Life and fate and an early catastrophe were ever at his heels, and when he at last falls fighting, sinks down in the very act of valour, the "happy ending," as he calls it for some of his correspondents, is, though precipitated and not conventional, essentially given us.

His descent and his origin all contribute to the picture, which it seems to me could scarce — since we speak of "endings" — have had a better beginning had he himself prearranged it. Without prearrangements indeed it was such a cluster of terms as could never be wasted on him, one of those innumerable matters of "effect," Scotch and other, that helped to fill his romantic consciousness.

Edinburgh, in the first place, the "romantic town," was as much his "own" as it ever was the great precursor's whom, in "Weir of Hermiston" as well as elsewhere, he presses so hard; and this even in spite of continual absence — in virtue of a constant imaginative reference and an intense intellectual possession. The immediate background formed by the profession of his family — the charge of the public lights on northern coasts — was a setting that he could not have seen his way to better; while no less happy a condition was met by his being all lonely in his father's house — the more that the father, admirably commemorated by the son and after his fashion as strongly marked, was antique and strenuous, and that the son, a genius to be and of frail constitution, was (in the words of the charming anecdote of an Edinburgh lady retailed in one of these volumes), if not exactly what could be called bonny, "pale, penetrating and interesting." The poet in him had from the first to be pacified — temporarily, that is, and from hand to mouth, as is the manner for poets; so that with friction and tension playing their part, with the filial relation quite classically troubled, with breaks of tradition and lapses from faith, with restless excursions and sombre returns, with the love of life at large mixed in his heart with every sort of local piety and passion and the unjustified artist fermenting on top of all in the recusant engineer, he was as well started as possible toward the character he was to keep.

All this obviously, however, was the sort of thing that the story the most generally approved would have had at heart to represent as the mere wild oats of a slightly uncanny cleverness — as the life handsomely reconciled in time to the common course and crowned, after a fling or two of amusement, with young wedded love and civic responsibility. The actual story, alas, was to transcend the conventional one, for it happened to be a case of a hero of too long a wind and too well turned out for his part. Everything was right for the discipline of Alan Fairford but that the youth *was* after all a phoenix. As soon as it became a case of justifying himself for straying — as in the enchanting "Inland Voyage" and the "Travels with a Donkey" — how was he to escape doing so with supreme felicity? The fascination in him from the first is the mixture, and the extraordinary charm of his letters is that they are always showing this. It is the proportions moreover that are so admirable — the quantity of each different thing that he fitted to each other one and to the whole. The free life would have been all his dream if so large a part of it had not been that love of letters, of expression and form, which is but another name for the life of service. Almost the last word about him, by the same law, would be that he had at any rate consummately written, were it not that he seems still better characterised by his having at any rate supremely lived.

Perpetually and exquisitely amusing as he was, his ambiguities and compatibilities yielded, for all the wear and tear of them, endless "fun" even to himself; and no one knew so well with what linked diversities he was saddled or, to put it the other way, how many horses he had to drive at once. It took his own delightful talk to show how more than absurd it might be, and, if convenient, how very obscurely so, that such an incurable rover should have been complicated both with such an incurable scribbler and such an incurable invalid, and that a man should find himself such an anomaly as a drenched yachtsman haunted with "style," a shameless Bohemian haunted with duty, and a victim at once of the personal hunger and instinct for adventure and of the critical, constructive, sedentary view of it. He had everything all round — adventure most of all; to feel which we have only to turn from the beautiful flush of it in his text to the scarce less beautiful vision of the great hilltop in Pacific seas to which he was borne after death by islanders and chiefs. Fate, as if to distinguish him as handsomely as possible, seemed to be ever treating him to some chance for an act or a course that had almost nothing in its favour but its inordinate difficulty. If the difficulty was in these cases not *all* the beauty for him it at least never prevented his finding it — or our finding, at any rate, as observers — so much beauty as comes from a great risk accepted either for an idea or for simply joy. The joy of risks, the more personal the better, was never far from him, any more than the excitement of ideas. The most important step in his life was a signal instance of this, as we may discern in the light of "The Amateur Emigrant" and "Across the Plains," the report of the conditions in which he fared from England to California to be married. Here as always the great note is the heroic mixture — the thing he *saw*, morally as well as

R.L.S. Dictating to Belle

imaginatively; action and performance at any cost, and the cost made immense by want of health and want of money, illness and anxiety of the extremest kind, and by unsparing sensibilities and perceptions. He had been launched in the world for a fighter with the organism say of a "composer," though also it must be added with a beautiful saving sanity.

It is doubtless after his settlement in Samoa that his letters have most to give, but there are things they throw off from the first that strike the note above all characteristic, show his imagination always at play, for drollery or philosophy, with his circumstances. The difficulty in writing of him under the personal impression is to suggest enough how directly his being the genius that he was kept counting in it. In 1879 he writes from Monterey to Mr Edmund Gosse, in reference to certain grave symptoms of illness: "I may be wrong, but . . . I believe I must go . . . But death is no bad friend; a few aches and gasps, and we are done; like the truant child, I am beginning to grow weary and timid in this big, jostling city, and could run to my nurse, even although she should have to whip me before putting me to bed." This charming renunciation expresses itself at the very time his talent was growing finer; he was so fond of the sense of youth and the idea of play that he saw whatever happened to him in images and figures, in the terms almost of the sports of childhood. "Are you coming over again to see me some day soon? I keep returning, and now hand over fist, from the realms of Hades. I saw that gentleman between the eyes, and fear him less after each visit. Only Charon and his rough boatmanship I somewhat fear."

The fear remained with him, sometimes greater, sometimes less, during the first years after his marriage, those spent abroad and in England in health resorts, and it marks constantly, as one may say, one end of the range of his humour — the humour always busy at the other end with the impatience of timidities and precautions and the vision and invention of essentially open-air situations. It was the possibility of the open-air situation that at last appealed to him as the cast worth staking all for — on which, as usual in his admirable rashnesses, he was extraordinarily justified. "No man but myself knew all my bitterness in those days. Remember that, the next time you think I regret my exile . . . Remember the pallid brute that lived in Skerryvore like a weevil in a biscuit."

He found after an extraordinarily adventurous quest the treasure island, the climatic paradise that met, that enhanced his possibilities; and with this discovery was ushered in his completely full and rich period, the time in which — as the wondrous whimsicality and spontaneity of his correspondence testify — his genius and his character most overflowed. He had done as well for himself in his appropriation of Samoa as if he had done it for the hero of a novel, only with the complications and braveries actual and palpable. "I have no more hope in anything" — and this in the midst of magnificent production — "than a dead frog; I go into everything with a composed despair, and don't mind — just as I always go to sea with the conviction I am to be drowned, and like it before all other pleasures." He could go to sea as often as he liked and not be spared such hours as one of these pages vividly evokes — those of the joy of fictive composition in

an otherwise prostrating storm, amid the crash of the elements and with his grasp of his subject but too needfully sacrificed, it might have appeared, to his clutch of seat and inkstand. "If only I could secure a violent death, what a fine success! I wish to die in my boots; no more Land of Counterpane for me. To be drowned, to be shot, to be thrown from a horse — aye, to be hanged rather than pass again through that slow dissolution."

He speaks in one of the "Vailima Letters," Mr Colvin's publication of 1895, to which it is an office of these volumes promptly to make us return, of one of his fictions as a "long tough yarn with some pictures of the manners of to-day in the greater world — not the shoddy sham world of cities, clubs and colleges, but the world where men still live a man's life." That is distinct, and in the same letter he throws off a summary of all that in his final phase satisfied and bribed him which is as significant as it is racy. His correspondent, as was inevitable now and then for his friends at home, appears to have indulged in one of those harmless pointings of the moral — as to the distant dangers he *would* court — by which we all were more or less moved to relieve ourselves of the depressed consciousness that he could do beautifully without us and that our collective tameness was far (which indeed was distinctly the case) from forming his proper element. There is no romantic life for which something amiable has not to be sweepingly sacrificed, and of *us* in our inevitable category the sweep practically was clean.

> Your letter had the most wonderful "I told you so" I heard in the course of my life. Why, you madman, I wouldn't change my present installation for any post, dignity, honour, or advantage conceivable to me. It fills the bill; I have the loveliest time. And as for wars and rumours of wars, you surely know enough of me to be aware that I like that also a thousand times better than decrepit peace in Middlesex. I do not quite like politics. I am too aristocratic, I fear, for that. God knows I don't care who I chum with; perhaps like sailors best; but to go round and sue and sneak to keep a crowd together — never.

His categories satisfied him; he had got hold of "the world where men still live a man's life" — which was not, as we have just seen, that of "cities, clubs and colleges." He was supremely suited in short at last — at the cost, it was to be said, of simplifications of view that, intellectual-

Valima

ly, he failed quite exactly (it was one of his few limitations) to measure; but in a way that ministered to his rare capacity for growth and placed in supreme relief his affinity with the universal romantic. It was not that anything could ever be for him plain sailing, but that he had been able at forty to turn his life into the fairytale of achieving, in a climate that he somewhere describes as "an expurgated heaven", such a happy physical consciousness as he had never known. This enlarged in every way his career, opening the door still wider to that real puss-in-the-corner game of opposites by which we have critically the interest of seeing him perpetually agitated. Let me repeat that these new volumes, from the date of his definite expatriation, direct us for the details of the picture constantly to the "Vailima Letters;" with as constant an effect of our thanking our fortune — to say nothing of his own — that he should have had in these years a correspondent and a confidant who so beautifully drew him out. If he possessed in Mr Sidney Colvin his literary chargé d'affaires at home, the ideal friend and *alter ego* on whom he could unlimitedly rest, this is a proof the more — with the general rarity of such cases — of what it was in his nature to make people wish to do for him. To Mr Colvin he is more familiar than to any one, more whimsical and natural and frequently more inimitable — of all of which a just notion can be given only by abundant citation. And yet citation itself is embarrassed, with nothing to guide it but his perpetual spirits, perpetual acuteness and felicity, restlessness of fancy and of judgment. These things make him jump from pole to pole and fairly hum, at times, among the objects and subjects that filled his air, like a charged bee among flowers.

He is never more delightful than when he is most egotistic, most consciously charmed with something he has done.

> And the papers are some of them up to dick, and no mistake. I agree with you, the lights seem a little turned down.

When we learn that the articles alluded to are those collected in "Across the Plains" we quite assent to this impression made by them after a troubled interval, and envy the author who, in a far Pacific isle, could see "The Lantern Bearers," "A Letter to a Young Gentleman" and "Pulvis et Umbra" float back to him as a guarantee of his faculty and between covers constituting the book that is to live. Stevenson's masculine wisdom moreover, his remarkable final sanity, is always — and it was not what made least in him for happy intercourse — close to his comedy and next door to his slang.

> And however low the lights are, the stuff is true, and I believe the more effective; after all, what I wish to fight is the best fought by a rather cheerless presentation of the truth. The world must return some day to the word "duty," and be done with the word "reward." There are no rewards, and plenty duties. And the sooner a man sees that and acts upon it, like a gentleman or a fine old barbarian, the better for himself.

It would perhaps be difficult to quote a single paragraph giving more than that of the whole of him. But there is abundance of him in this too:

> How do journalists fetch up their drivel? . . . It has taken me two months to write 45,500 words; and, be damned to my wicked prowess, I am proud of the exploit! . . . A respectable little five-bob volume, to bloom unread in shop windows. After that I'll have a spank at fiction. And rest? I shall rest in the grave, or when I come to Italy. If only the public will continue to support me! I lost my chance not dying; there seems blooming little fear of it now. I worked close on five hours this morning; the day before, close on nine; and unless I finish myself off with this letter I'll have another hour and a half, or *aiblins twa*, before dinner. Poor man, how you must envy me as you hear of these orgies or work, and you scarce able for a letter. But Lord! Colvin, how lucky the situations are not reversed, for I have no situation, nor am fit for any. Life is a steigh brae. Here, have at Knappe, and no more clavers!

If he talked profusely — and this is perfect talk — if he loved to talk above all of his work in hand, it was because, though perpetually frail, he was never inert, and did a thing, if he did it at all, with passion. He was not fit, he says, for a situation, but a situation overtook him inexorably at Vailima, and doubtless at last indeed swallowed him up. His position, with differences, comparing in some respects smaller things to greater, and with fewer differences after all then likenesses, his position resembles that of Scott at Abbotsford, just as, sound, sensible and strong on each side in spite of the immense gift of dramatic and poetic vision, the earlier and the later man had something of a common nature. Life became bigger for each than the answering effort could meet, and in their death they were not divided. Stevenson's late emancipation was a fairytale only because he himself was in his manner a magician. He liked to handle many matters and to shrink from none; nothing can exceed the impression we get of the things that in these years he dealt with from day to day and as they came up, and the things that, as well, almost without order or relief, he planned and invented, took up and talked of and dropped, took up and talked of and carried through. Had I space to treat myself to a clue for selection from the whole record there is nothing I should better like it to be than a tracking of his "literary opinions" and literary projects, the scattered swarm of his views, sympathies, antipathies, *obiter dicta*, as an artist — his flurries and fancies, imaginations, evocations, quick infatuations, as a teller of possible tales. Here is a whole little circle of discussion, yet such a circle that to engage one's self at all is to be too much engulfed.

His overflow on such matters is meanwhile amusing enough as mere spirits and sport — interesting as it would yet be to catch as we might, at different moments, the congruity between the manner of his feeling a fable in the germ and that of his afterwards handling it. There are passages again and again that light strikingly what I should call his general conscious method in this relation, were I not more tempted to call it his conscious — for that is what it seems to come to — negation of method. A whole delightful letter — to Mr Colvin, February 1, 1892 — is a vivid type. (This letter, I may mention, is independently notable for the drollery of its allusion to a sense of scandal — of all things in the world — excited in some editorial breast by "The Beach of Falesà;" which leads him to the highly pertinent remark that "this is a poison bad world for the romancer, this Anglo-Saxon world; I usually get out of it by not having any women in it at all." Then he remembers he had "The Treasure of Franchard" refused as unfit for a family magazine and feels — as well he may — "despair weigh upon his wrists." The despair haunts him and comes out on another occasion. "Five more chapters of David . . . All love affair; seems pretty good to me. Will it do for the young person? I don't know: since the Beach, I know nothing except that men are fools and hypocrites, and I know less of them than I was fond enough to fancy.") Always a part of his physiognomy is the play, so particularly salient, of his moral fluctuations, the way his spirits are upset by his melancholy and his grand conclusions by his rueful doubts.

He communicates to his confidant with the eagerness of a boy confabulating in holidays over a Christmas charade; but I remember no instance of his expressing a subject, as one may say *as* a subject — hinting at what novelists mainly know, one would imagine, as the determinant thing in it, the idea out of which it springs. The form, the envelope, is there with him, headforemost, *as* the idea; titles, names, that is, chapters, sequences, orders, while we are still asking ourselves how it was that he primarily put to his own mind what it was all to be about. He simply *felt* this, evidently, and it is always the one dumb sound, the stopped pipe or only unexpressed thing, in all his contagious candour. He finds none the less in the letter to which I refer one of the problems of the wonderful projected "Sophia Scarlet" "exactly a Balzac one, and I wish I had his fist — for I have already a better method — the kinetic — whereas he continually allowed himself to be led into the static." There we have him — Stevenson, not Balzac — at his most overflowing, and after all radiantly capable of conceiving at another moment that his "better method" would have been none at all for Balzac's vision of a subject, least of all *the* subject, the whole of life. Balzac's method was adapted to his notion of presentation — which we may accept, it strikes me, under the protection of what he presents. Were it not, in fine, as I may repeat, to embark in a bigger boat that would here turn round I might note further that Stevenson has elsewhere — was disposed in general to have — too short a way with this master. There is an interesting passage in which he charges him with having never known what to leave out, a passage which has its bearing on condition of being read with due remembrance of the class of performance to which "Le Colonel Chabert," for instance, "Le Curé de Tours," "L'Interdiction," "La Messe de l'Athée" (to name but a few brief masterpieces in a long list) appertain.

These, however, are comparatively small questions; *the* impression, for the reader of the later letters, is simply one of singular beauty — of deepening talent, of happier and richer expression, and in especial of an ironic desperate gallantry that burns away, with a finer and finer fire, in a strange alien air and is only the more touching to us from his own resolute consumption of the smoke. He had incurred great charges, he sailed a ship loaded to the brim, so that the strain under which he lived and wrought was immense; but the very grimness of it all is sunny, slangy, funny, familiar; there is as little of the florid in his flashes of melancholly as of the really grey under stress of his wisdom. This wisdom had sometimes on matters of art, I think, its lapses, but on matters of life it was really winged and inspired. He has a soundness as to questions of the vital connection, a soundness all liberal and easy and born of the manly experience, that it is a luxury to touch. There are no compunctions nor real impatiences, for he had in a singular degree got what he wanted, the life absolutely discockneyfied, the situation as romantically "swagger" as if it had been imagination made real; but his practical anxieties necessarily spin themselves finer, and it is just this production of the thing imagined that had more and more to meet them. It all hung, the situation, by *that* beautiful golden thread, the swinging of which in the winds, as he spins it in alternate doubt and elation, we watch with much of the suspense and pity with which we sit at the serious drama. It is serious in the extreme; yet the forcing of production, in the case of a faculty so beautiful and delicate, affects us almost as the straining of a nerve or the distortion of a feature.

> I sometimes sit and yearn for anything in the nature of an income that would come in — mine had all got to be gone and fished for with the immortal mind of man. What I want is the income that really comes in of itself, while all you have to do is just to blossom and exist and sit on chairs . . . I should probably amuse myself with works that would make your hair curl, if you had any left.

To read over some of his happiest things, to renew one's sense of the extraordinarily fine temper of his imagination, is to say to one's self "What a horse to have to ride every week to market!" We must all go to market, but the most fortunate of us surely are those who may drive thither, and on days not too frequent, nor by a road too rough, a ruder and homelier animal. He touches in more than one place — and with notable beauty and real authority in that little mine of felicities the "Letter to a Young Gentleman" — on the conscience for "frugality" which should be the artist's finest point of honour; so that one of his complications here was undoubtedly the sense that on this score his position had inevitably become somewhat false. The literary romantic is by no means necessarily expensive, but of the many ways in which the practical, the active, has to be paid for this depature from frugality would be, it is easy to conceive, not the least. And we perceive his recognising this as he recognised everything — if not in time, then out of it; accepting inconsistency, as he always did, with the gaiety of a man of courage — not being, that is, however intelligent, priggish for logic and the grocer's book any more than for anything else. Only everything made for keeping it up, and it was a great deal to keep up; though when he throws off "The Ebb-Tide" and rises to "Catriona," and then again to "Weir of Hermiston," as if he could rise to almost anything, we breathe anew and looking longingly forward. The latest of these letters contain such admirable

things, testify so to the reach of his intelligence and in short vibrate so with genius and charm, that we feel him at moments not only unexhausted but replenished, and capable perhaps, for all we know to the contrary, of new experiments and deeper notes. The intelligence and attention are so fine that he misses nothing from unawareness; not a gossamer thread of the "thought of the time" that, wafted to him on the other side of the globe, may not be caught in a branch and played with; he puts such a soul into nature and such human meanings, for comedy and tragedy, into what surrounds him, however shabby or short, that he really lives in society by living in his own perceptions and generosities or, as we say nowadays, his own atmosphere. In this atmosphere — which seems to have had the gift of abounding the more it was breathed by others — these pages somehow prompt us to see almost every object on his tropic isle bathed and refreshed.

So far at any rate from growing thin for want of London he can transmit to London or to its neighbourhood communications such as it would scarce know otherwise where to seek. A letter to his cousin, R. A. M. Stevenson, of September 1894, touches so on all things and, as he would himself have said, so adorns them, brimming over with its happy extravagance of thought, that, far again from our feeling Vailima, in the light of it, to be out of the world, it strikes us that the world has moved for the time to Vailima. There is world enough everywhere, he quite unconsciously shows, for the individual, the right one, to be what we call a man of it. He has, like every one not convenienced with the pleasant back-door of stupidity, to make his account with seeing and facing more things, seeing and facing everything, with the unrest of new impressions and ideas, the loss of the fond complacencies of youth.

> But as I go on in life, day by day, I become more of a bewildered child; I cannot get used to this world, to procreation, to heredity, to sight, to hearing; the commonest things are a burthen. The prim obliterated polite face of life, and the broad, bawdy and orgiastic — or maenadic — foundations, form a spectacle to which no habit reconciles me; and "I could wish my days to be bound each to each" by the same open-mouthed wonder. They are anyway, and whether I wish it or not . . . I remember very

R.L.S. and Fanny on the *Janet Nicol*

well your attitude to life — this conventional surface of it. You have none of that curiosity for the social stage directions, the trivial *ficelles* of the business; it is simian; but that is how the wild youth of man is captured.

The whole letter is enchanting.

But no doubt there is something great in the half success that has attended the effort of turning into an emotional region Bald Conduct without any appeal, or almost none, to the figurative, mysterious and constitutive facts of life. Not that conduct is not constitutive, but dear! it's dreary! On the whole, conduct is better dealt with on the cast-iron "gentleman" and duty formula, with as little fervour and poetry as possible; stoical and short.

The last letter of all, it will have been abundantly noted, has, with one of those characteristically thrown-out references to himself that were always half a whim, half a truth and all a picture, a remarkable premonition. It is addressed to Mr Edmund Gosse.

> It is all very well to talk of renunciation, and of course it has to be done. But for my part, give me a roaring toothache! I do like to be deceived and to dream, but I have very little use for either watching or meditation. I was not born for age . . . I am a childless, rather bitter, very clear-eyed, blighted youth. I have, in fact, lost the path that makes it easy and natural for you to descend the hill. I am going at it straight. And where I have to go down it is a precipice . . . You can never write another dedication that can give the same pleasure to the vanished Tusitala.

Two days later he met his end in the happiest form, by the straight swift bolt of the gods. It was, as all his readers know, with an admirable unfinished thing in hand, scarce a quarter written — a composition as to which his hopes were, presumably with much justice and as they were by no means always, of the highest. Nothing is more interesting than the rich way in which, in "Weir of Hermiston" and "Catriona," the predominant imaginative Scot reasserts himself after gaps and lapses, distractions and deflections superficially extreme. There are surely few backward jumps of this energy more joyous and à pieds joints, or of a kind more interesting to a critic. The imaginative vision is hungry and tender just in proportion as the actual is otherwise beset; so that we must sigh always in vain for the quality that this purified flame, as we call it, would have been able to give the metal. And how many things for the critic the case suggests — how many possible reflections cluster about it and seem to take light from it! It was "romance" indeed, "Weir of Hermiston." we feel, as we see it only grow in assurance and ease when the reach to it over all the spaces becomes more positively artificial. The case is literary to intensity, and, given the nature of the talent, only thereby the more beautiful: he embroiders in silk and silver — in defiance of climate and nature, of every near aspect, and with such another antique needle as was nowhere, least of all in those latitudes, to be bought — in the intervals of wondrous international and insular politics and of fifty material cares and complications. His special stock of association, most personal style and most unteachable trick fly away again to him like so many strayed birds to nest, each with the flutter in its beak of some scrap of document or legend, some fragment of picture or story, to be retouched, revarnished and reframed.

These things he does with a gusto, moreover, for which it must be granted that his literary treatment of the islands and the island life had ever vainly waited. Curious enough that his years of the tropics and his fraternity with the natives never drew from him any such "rendered" view as might have been looked for in advance. For the absent and vanished Scotland he has the image — within the limits (too narrow ones we may perhaps judge) admitted by his particular poetic; but the law of these things in him was, as of many others, amusingly conscientiously perverse. The Pacific, in which he materially delighted, made him "descriptively" serious and even rather dry; with his own country, on the other hand, materially impossible, he was ready to tread an endless measure. He easily sends us back again here to our vision of his mixture. There was only one thing on earth that he loved as much as literature — which was the total absense of it; and to the present, the immediate, whatever it was, he always made the latter offering. Samoa was susceptible of no "style" — none of that, above all, with which he was most conscious of an affinity — save the demonstration of its rightness for life; and this left the field abundantly clear for the Border, the Great North Road and the eighteenth century. I have been reading over "Catriona" and "Weir" with the purest pleasure with which we can follow a man of genius — that of seeing him abound in his own sense. In "Weir" especially, like an improvising pianist, he super-abounds and revels, and his own sense, by a happy stroke, appeared likely never more fully and brightly to justify him; to have become even in some degree a new sense, with new chords and possibilities. It is the "old game," but it is the old game that he exquisitely understands. The figure of Hermiston is creative work of the highest order, those of the two Kirsties, especially that of the elder, scarce less so; and we ache for the loss of a thing which could give out such touches as the quick joy, at finding herself in falsehood, of the enamoured girl whose brooding elder brother had told her that as soon as she has a lover she will begin to lie (" 'Will I have gotten my jo now?' she thought with secret rapture"); or a passage so richly charged with imagination as that in which the young lover recalls her as he has first seen and desired her, seated at grey of evening on an old tomb in the moorland and unconsciously making him think, by her scrap of song, both of his mother, who sang it and whom he has lost, and

> of their common ancestors now dead, of their rude wars composed, their weapons buried with them, and of these strange changelings, their descendants, who lingered a little in their places and would soon be gone also, and perhaps sung of by others at the gloaming hour. By one of the unconscious arts of tenderness the two women were enshrined together in his memory. Tears, in that hour of sensibility, came into his eyes indifferently at the thought of either; and the girl, from being something merely bright and shapely, was caught up into the zone of things serious as life and death and his dead mother. So that, in all ways and on either side, Fate played his game artfully with this poor pair of children. The generations were prepared, the pangs were made ready, before the curtain rose on the dark drama.

It is not a tribute that Stevenson would at all have appreciated, but I may not forbear noting how closely such a page recalls many another in the tenderest manner of Pierre Loti. There would not, compared, be a pin to choose between them. How, we at all events ask ourselves as we consider "Weir," could he have kept it up? — while the reason for which he didn't reads itself back into his text as a kind of beautiful rash divination in him that he mightn't have to. Among prose fragments it stands quite alone, with the particular grace and sanctity of mutilation worn by the marble morsels of masterwork in another art. This and the other things of his best he left; but these things, lovely as, on rereading many of them at the suggestion of his Correspondence, they are, are not the whole, nor more than the half, of his abiding charm. The finest papers in "Across the Plains," in "Memories and Portraits," in "Virginibus Puerisque," stout of substance and supremely silver of speech, have both a nobleness and a nearness that place them, for perfection and roundness, above his fictions, and that also may well remind a vulgarised generation of what, even under its nose, English prose can be. But it is bound up with his name, for our wonder and reflection, that he is something other than the author of this or that particular beautiful thing, or of all such things together. It has been his fortune (whether or no the greatest that can befall a man of letters) to have had to consent to become, by a process not purely mystic and not wholly untraceable — what shall we call it? — a Figure. Tracing is needless now, for the personality has acted and the incarnation is full. There he is — he has passed ineffaceably into happy legend. This case of the figure is of the rarest and the honour surely of the greatest. In all our literature we can count them, sometimes with the work and sometimes without. The work has often been great and yet the figure *nil*. Johnson was one, and Goldsmith and Byron; and the two former moreover not in any degree, like Stevenson, in virtue of the element of grace. Was it this element that fixed the claim even for Byron? It seems doubtful; and the list at all events as we approach our own day shortens and stops. Stevenson has it at present — may we not say? — pretty well to himself, and it is not one of the scrolls in which he least will live.

Stevenson and America

J.C. FURNAS

In Stevenson's time the United States had long bulked large in British consciousness. British leaders of several social and political persuasions anxiously observed such American developments as manhood suffrage, relatively easy divorce, relatively ready economic opportunity, discouragement of class distinctions and disestablishment of religion. For a generation there had been a consequent flood of books — a few valuable, the rest tendentiously partisan — about how such innovations were working out across the Atlantic. The gravitational pull of the new nation drew a steady flow of emigration thither out of London, Liverpool and Glasgow as well as out of Ireland. It included not only the land- and job-hungry but also visionaries seeking a favourable soil for social experiment, such as Fanny Wright, Morris Birkbeck, Robert Dale Owen . . .

By the mid-century other poignant issues flavoured British associations with the name 'America'. The pocketbook nerve was painfully wrung when British investors, many of them influential and articulate, found several States of the Union defaulting on their bonds — for which, ignorant of the nature of the Union, they blamed the whole nation. British humanitarians followed with vast sympathy — and, it must be admitted, some Pharisaism — the battle of their American opposite numbers against black slavery. By the sixth decade of the century the conflict had festered into the great Civil War that directly threatened Britain's economy and some-times caused otherwise responsible persons on both sides of the water to conceive of a third Anglo-American war as not impossible.

All that and more necessarily impinged on an alert, well-connected youngster in Edinburgh. He once wrote how 'For many years America was to me a sort of promised land . . . [to which] the minds of young men in England turn naturally at a certain hopeful period . . . imagine a young man . . . grown up in an old and rigid circle, following bygone fashions and taught to distrust his own fresh instincts, and who now suddenly hears of a family of cousins, all about his own age, who keep house together by themselves and live far from restraint and tradition . . . It seems to [him] that out west the war of life was still conducted in the open air, and on free barbaric terms . . . not yet . . . by compromise, costume, forms of procedure, and sad, senseless, self-denial.'

The results of Louis Stevenson divide conveniently into two groups: the first from hearsay and reading at long range, the second from immediate contact. For 150 years heavy emigration from Scotland had been enriching America with inflowing skills, institutions and attitudes. As far as I know, however, the only personal connection between Stevenson's forebears — civil engineers on one side, ministers on the other — and the new nation was a visit made by an engineer uncle, David Stevenson, in the 1830s to inspect American engineering feats. He wrote an able book about what my countrymen were doing with fast steamboats, wooden covered bridges across river gorges, canal-barges lifted over thousand foot summits on inclined planes. His book was reprinted thirty years later to help young engineers facing cognate problems in India. No doubt it was included in Thomas Stevenson's family library at 17 Heriot Row. But in view of the family's failure to make an engineer out of young Louis, one may doubt that he paid its content much heed, if indeed he ever opened it.

We do know that that library contained *Uncle Tom's Cabin* and that as a boy Louis read it eagerly. He was probably well prepared for its melodramatic distortions by his childhood fascination with the America depicted by the watery imitators of James Fenimore Cooper then infesting the popular press on both sides of the Atlantic. This was well before the Wild West tradition, the scalp-lifting, bow-and-arrow, noble-savage and heap-big-paleface sort of thing — about as good preparation for the real America as a performance of *The Tempest* would be for a visit to Bermuda. When, in 1879, Louis awakened in an

Reunion House

American rail-road car actually to find himself in the State of Ohio, he recalled how, 'I have played at being in Ohio by the week, and enjoyed some capital sport there with a dummy gun . . . [inspired by] a work which appeared in *Cassell's Family Paper* . . . read aloud to me by my nurse . . . the doings of one Custaloga, an Indian brave, who, in the last chapter . . . washed the paint off his face and became Sir Reginald Somebody-or-other, a trick

I never forgave him . . .' And in parallel here in Midwestern actuality the woods in which that noble savage had run had tamely given way to fields of man-high corn, and what Stevenson called, 'long aerial vistas . . . clean, bright, gardened townships . . . a sort of flat paradise . . .'

Custaloga's Ohio was a Neverneverland that the boy Louis shared with thousands of other boy-children reared among, and by, the Victorian upper classes. Toward the end of his second decade he moved beyond most of them by exploring Hawthorne, Poe, Whitman and probably other American writers so eagerly that while at the University he read to the Speculative Society a paper maintaining with more generosity than judgment that the fertility of American literature already equalled Britain's. Scholastic ingenuity could trace in his subsequent work influences from Poe certainly, from Hawthorne probably. But such consequences were dwarfed by the impact on him of Walt Whitman. True, the America depicted in *Leaves of Grass* is no more reliable than the Ohio of *Cassell's Family Paper* or the Louisiana of *Uncle Tom's Cabin* — which shows all too abjectly that Mrs Stowe had never been anywhere near either Louisiana or a cotton plantation. But that is impertinent to the importance of Whitman in Stevenson's young life — probably greater for him, the neophyte, than for the established men of letters then making Whitman an object of fashionable acclaim among the dutifully sensitive.

Even without direct evidence one deduces that from some of his early verses. Naturally he found an essentially American quality in Whitman's fascination with the bare word Democracy and unlimited belief in the future of his country. Nor was this feeling wrong. The American brashness is indubitably there. On the literary side he responded as cordially as Swinburne to the throbbing beauties of 'When Lilacs Last in the Door Yard Bloomed', but the chief point here is the statement made several years later in a self-examining mood that his hope of personal integration in his early twenties came of three things: 'natural growth, the coming of friends, and the study of Walt Whitman'. Presently he is even advising parents and guardians to administer Whitman as a specific for the distressing malady of being seventeen years old . . .

That prescription means that the floundering youngster had found sympathy and guidance in Whitman's sometimes explicit doctrine that the human being robs himself of the juices of life unless he looks at everything, even a hair on the back of his hand, as if seeing it for the first time, never to see it again. This has mystical overtones and is really a counsel of despair, for anybody managing that too often in a given twenty-four hours would blissfully disintegrate. For young Louis' temperament, this teaching undergirded and accelerated an already marked bent for a hyper-perception imperatively demanding verbal expression. The causal order there is intentional. Primarily Louis Stevenson was a writer. He had in unusual degree the writer's urge so to handle language that its intrinsic glory and shrewdness sing together; and he already knew, or sensed, that vividly apprehended materials rank high among the nutrients of worthy writing. The relation is as old as Wordsworth's daffodils. But in Stevenson's case it was the American Whitman who probably did most to steer his finicky self-consciousness into an aesthetic usefulness. True, he might have managed some such thing on his own. But emphatic help at the right time was certainly handy and may have been crucial.

Other, more personal help came of Whitman's being, as Stevenson skilfully described him, 'the declared enemy of all reflex action, of all that is done between sleeping and waking, of all the pleasureless and imaginary duties in which we coin away our hearts . . . [Whitman preaches] a superior prudence, which has little or nothing in common with the maxims of the copy-book'. Very probably young Louis already mistrusted and disliked facile conformity before he even met Whitman. There was support in Burns, for instance, and among Edinburgh's local bohemians whom he deliberately cultivated, but, here again, Whitman was at least abetting, very possibly helping to create Stevenson's temperamental drift. This doctrine of a solipsist morality, a sort of romantic parallel to the Quaker doctrine of the Inner Light, came most fittingly from America where, one understood, democratic law and equalitarian sentiment both held that any one man — and so his spontaneous ways of doing and feeling — was as good as another. Never mind that most European observers of the day agreed that an abject

TREASURE ISLAND;
OR,
THE MUTINY OF THE HISPANIOLA.

By CAPTAIN GEORGE NORTH.

PROLOGUE.—THE ADMIRAL BENBOW.

CHAPTER I.

THE OLD SEA DOG AT THE ADMIRAL BENBOW.

SQUIRE TRELAWNEY, Dr. Livesey, and the rest of these gentlemen having asked me to write down the whole particulars about Treasure Island, from the beginning to the end, keeping nothing back but the bearings of the island, and that only because there is still treasure not yet lifted, I take up my pen in the year of grace 17—, and go back to the time when my father kept the Admiral Benbow Inn, and the brown old seaman, with the sabre cut, first took up his lodging under our roof.

I remember him as if it were yesterday, as he came plodding to the inn door, his sea-chest following behind him in a hand-barrow; a tall, strong, heavy, nut-brown man; his tarry pig-tail falling over the shoulders of his soiled blue coat; his hands ragged and scarred, with black, broken nails; and the sabre cut across one cheek, a dirty, livid white. I remember him looking round the cove and whistling to himself as he did so, and then breaking out in that old sea-song that he sang so often afterwards:

" Fifteen men on the dead man's chest—
Yo-ho-ho, and a bottle of rum,"

in the high, old tottering voice that seemed to have been tuned and broken at the capstan bars. Then he rapped on the door with a bit of stick like a hand-

walking the plank, and storms at sea, and the Dry Tortugas, and wild deeds and places in the Spanish Main. By his own account he must have lived his life among the wickedest fiends of men that ever sailed upon the sea; and the language in which he told these stories shocked our plain country people almost as much as the crimes that he described. My father was always saying the inn would be ruined, for people would soon cease coming there to be tyrannized over and put down, and sent shivering to their beds; but I really believe his presence did us good. People were frightened at the time, but on looking back they rather liked it; it was a fine excitement in a quiet country life; and there was even a party of the younger men who pretended to admire him, calling him a "true sea-dog," and a "real old salt," and such like names, and saying there was

TREASURE ISLAND.—"THE CAPTAIN AIMED AT THE FUGITIVE ONE LAST BLOW, WHICH, HOWEVER, WAS STOPPED BY THE SIGN BOARD."

last broke out with a villanous, low oath: "Silence, there, between decks!"

"Were you addressing me, sir?" says the doctor; and when the ruffian had told him, with another oath, that this was so, "I have only one thing to say to you, sir," replies the doctor, "that if you keep on drinking rum, the world will soon be quit of a very dirty, low scoundrel!"

The old fellow's fury was awful. He sprang to his feet, drew and opened a sailor's clasp-knife, and, balancing it open on the palm of his hand, threatened to pin the doctor to the wall. The doctor never so much as moved. He spoke to him, as before, over his shoulder, and in the same tone of voice; rather high, so that all the room might hear, but perfectly calm and steady:

"If you do not put that knife this instant in your

Young Folks serialisation of *Treasure Island*

---

conformity in dress, speech, opinions and behaviour was Americans' besetting sin. It probably was. In one or another set of terms that holds good of most societies. Indeed this trait made America all the better foil for Whitman's benevolent protest by precept and example against Mrs Grundy. Where better to find promising

antibodies than in the bloodstream of the patient with the most acute infection?

The sense of social release consequent on such teaching greatly appealed to a youngster already sniffing that sort of breeze. The same applies to his response to Henry David Thoreau — a figure not quite so peculiarly

American yet so inbued with the traits of the stereotype New England Yankee that the national reference is justified. The sage of Walden Pond was as non-conformist as Whitman if less rhapsodic about it, and just as confident that this was no mere matter of individual taste but a way to save one's soul alive. Stevenson truly said: '. . . it is what Thoreau whispers that Whitman so uproariously bawls' — that is, the spiritual duty of heightened awareness — and went on: 'The seeming significance of nature's appearances, their unchanging strangeness to the senses, and the thrilling response which they awake in the mind of man, continued to surprise and stimulate his spirits.' Neither sympathy with all this, nor pleasure in the writing skill of this American great master of pithy English could reconcile Louis to the priggishness that he smelled in Thoreau's cult of oneself. The suspicion had grounds. It was recently reenforced in the 1960's when this gaunt prophet of self-exploration, amateur asceticism and civil disobedience was canonized by young Americans committed to self-righteous life-styles and what has since been called the Cult of Me. Though grateful for help against what he took to be the toxins of convention, though bracketing Thoreau with Whitman in America's anticipation of a more rewarding world, young Louis nevertheless wanted more generosity stirred into his moral and intellectual Dutch courage. For that reason a third highly American phenomenon, Benjamin Franklin, caused him dismay mingled with derision. He never published nor, so far as I know, finished the essay on Franklin that he worked on during his momentous winter in San Francisco. I wish he had. The tenor of his odd references to Franklin in other writings makes it likely that on this subject he would have been at least as penetrating and far better reading than either Max Weber or D.H. Lawrence.

A parallel may occur here — Lawrence read much the same American writers that Stevenson knew and roughed out much of his famous *Studies in Classical American Literature* before he ever saw America. Both men let most of a decade elapse between such reading and actual experience of the country in question. And both had most of that experience not in the representative contexts of Main Street or Boston's Beacon Hill or New York's Broadway or The South's Magnolia Plantation but in offbeat areas: Lawrence in the artificial, Indian-obsessed artists' colony in New Mexico; Stevenson in post-Gold Rush California. After that, however, as so often happens, the parallel fails. Without being at all expert on Lawrence one can safely say that though New Mexico gave him fresh materials, it did nothing to mature his personality; whereas Stevenson came out of actual contact with his segment of the New World well on his way to the considerable maturity that he attained before he died in his mid-forties.

His first intimately fruitful acquaintance with Americans — and of a most congenial stripe — came in his mid-twenties when he was frequenting the artists' colonies in Paris and the Forest of Fontainebleau. In American art students he saw much the same variations in talent and integrity that appeared in their British comrades then numerous at Barbizon, an atmosphere faithfully described in early essays and in several sections of a much later novel, *The Wrecker*. He made fast friends with several Americans there, particularly with Will H. Low, eventually a well accepted illustrator and muralist. Most momentously it was there, that he met Fanny Van de Grift Osbourne, the American art student for whose sake he would go adventuring to California and who, as his wife, sickroom-guardian, executive officer and literary aide, was the chief reason for the American motif in his scenario.

No doubt the fact that Stevenson's wife was born and reared in my home town, Indianapolis, should help me to understand her. Indeed a second cousin of hers taught me Latin in high school, but the rawly new, artificially located settlement that produced her 150 years ago was only hoping to become the city I grew up in. Besides, she had a confusingly tangled temperament that unhappily eventuated in something like intermittent psychosis. For most of her life, however, she was a usefully formidable little woman of brisk good looks, incisive charm — for those who felt it — fierce loyalty, a great conceit of herself, the courage to disregard Mrs Grundy, and minor but genuine talents in writing and the graphic arts. When she met Louis she was encumbered by an estranged husband in California, where she had spent most of her married life before coming to Europe to study art, fetching along an almost grown-up daughter and an adolescent son. Those

Saranac Lake

three Americans became Louis' acquired family closely involved in his later career. Fanny was literary sounding-board, sometimes collaborator, and handled most of the logistics of his experience in the South Seas. Lloyd Osbourne, the stepson, was not only the occasion of *Treasure Island* but also collaborator on later work. Isobel (Osbourne) Strong, the step-daughter, was off and on her mother's barefoot second-in-command of the South Seas household and, as Louis' trusted amanuensis, was taking his dictation a few hours before he died.

American mother and American daughter, in Stevenson's view, shared valuable traits unfamiliar in Edinburgh's terms:

> . . . From European womankind
> They are divided and defined
> By the free limb and the plain mind,
> The nobler gait, and naked foot,
> The indiscreeter petticoat . . .

By then, of course, the American catalyst had been working a dozen years. For it was Fanny's being based in America that took him there for immersion in drastically solidifying experience. By that I mean not his marriage — though that played a part — but the transmuting, reality-imposing ordeal there inflicted on him, to his eventual benefit, by sickness and lack of money and certain other harshnesses that the America of 1879 showered on him.

He was twenty-eight years old when Fanny sent him that cable begging him to come to California to help her. Nobody knows in what words she couched her confused emotions and financial distress but it set Louis on his way with very slender resources. At that age most educated persons are getting their feet under them. So far, however, Louis had had only one settled purpose — to be a writer — and one settling encouragement — getting enough of his writing printed to show he was on the right track. Beyond that he remained too much like Henry James' casual depiction of him at the time: '. . . a pleasant fellow, but a shirt-collarless Bohemian, and a good deal (in an inoffensive way) of a poseur'. It is significant that when they met again — several years later, after Louis had been to America and back — they became fast friends on a basis of high mutual respect. In mid-1879 the dilettante choosing among the flavours of lie was too much to the fore. The young Stevenson rejoiced in going gypsying without a spare shirt; but instead of wearing his shirt dirtier and dirtier, he counted on throwing it away and buying another with the money that his father often supplied. He made his Inland Voyage to get material for a charming book about the joys and hardships of canoeing on French waterways; but when the cold and wet grew too onerous, he had only to find the nearest railroad station and buy a ticket to conventional comfort.

Similarly he also planned to write about his trip to rescue Fanny, but he travelled on the cheap in below-decks squalor next to a mass of impecunious America-bound emigrants not because such circumstances promised better copy but because he could afford nothing else. Soon his native good will and skill in personal relations had him on good terms with the steerage and gathering unexpected knowledge about those proto-Americans and by implication, the country they were going to. Though decent enough, most of those emigrant Scots and English were no valiant freedom-seekers bent on building up a glorious new nation and filling their broad chests with New World air. Instead they proved to be misfits or failures or feckless losers leaving a country they could not cope with in vague hopes that the new one would be less exacting. Here was new light on Whitman's 'O Pioneers!', and all that. His equalitarian leanings and social good taste kept him from putting on airs, which earned him the healthy discovery that in consequence nobody took him for anything out of the ordinary in steerage terms. His self-conscious forays into Edinburgh's seamy side had not altogether prepared him for that — which made the joke both better and more educational.

More low-keyed hardship in New York sent him on westward — on wheels now, in cheap railroad cars packed with more emigrants, part-American, part exotic, a similarly motivated westward drift of the same kinds of men, women and children. What with fatigue, poor and scanty nourishment and doubtless the strain of wondering what turmoil awaited him in California, he was by no means well, but as a veteran of sickness for half his young life he managed to keep up the journal that would turn into books about this strange journey. The exultation of leaving the western desert for the vigorous, handsome fertility of Northern California picked him up for a while, but Fanny's affairs — now inextricably his own — were quite as vexing as expected. A welter of indecision and misunderstandings sent him on a solitary camping trip in the hills to recover equilibrium. Up there all alone he fell into a semi-comatose sickness and was close to death when a pair of prospectors found him and played ministering angels until he could creep back to civilization and problems again. If his life story had an identifiable turning point, that was it.

South Sea feast

First in the Mexican-flavoured old capital village of Monterey, later in San Francisco, he made friends of polyglot fellow boarders, explored Monterey beach and the San Francisco waterfront, endured the vacillations of Fanny's plans for divorce and marriage — and worked at his trade through better and worse health. Though often a very sick man, he was never again quite as ill as he had been up in the hills. Nor was his work ever again as self-centred as it had been. Something about six thousand miles of sordid pilgrimage among strangers plus a brush with death seems to have effected a sea-and-land change. In token of it the small books made out of his journal — *The Amateur Emigrant* and *Across the Plains* — have a new energy and pith. The *Emigrant* was not published in his lifetime because the change in tone alarmed his family and his literary mentors alike. Thomas Stevenson bought back the copyright before it could get into print. One is tempted also to discern a soldier tone in his personal life even before the actual marriage in May, 1880, as well as to wonder what his writing would have been like had he never had occasion to pursue his lady so far across this hygienically traumatic new country.

Even in strictly literary terms Stevenson owed America much. For one thing it was American editors and publishers who, beginning in 1888, stirred by the sensation caused by *Dr Jekyll and Mr Hyde*, first paid him substantial sums for his work. Unlike most writing visitors, he followed his uncle's wise example and refrained from doing a synoptic book about the States. His writings on particular American localities are not only good samples of his new voice — the same and yet richer and steadier — but also indispensable glimpses of a California that vanished generations ago. The pertinent chapters in *The Wrecker*, for instance, outshine all other accounts of the San Francisco of his time. Monterey and the upper Napa Valley gave him the topography and flora of *Treasure Island*. The end of *The Master of Ballantrae*, though ill advised as structure, is a bleak tribute to the achingly bitter winters in America's Adirondack Mountains where the Stevensons spent a winter for the sake of his lungs. In *The Silverado Squatters*, about a stay in an abandoned mining camp in California, the new voice was in admirable form with genially generous portraits of the local poor whites, the local Shylock and the devoted wine-growers of the Napa Valley. The man who had written of Thoreau that, 'Like a child, he disliked the taste of wine — or perhaps, living in America, had never tasted any that was good . . .' now found promise of very worth while wine to come from these California vineyards. To Stevenson good wine was almost as important as sound writing, so doubtless this revision of unjustified assumptions helped to make up for Whitman's poor sociology. Here too swam into his ken what he called, 'the playful, innocuous American cocktail. I drank it and lo! veins of living fire ran down my leg; and then a focus of conflagration that remained seated in my stomach, not unpleasantly, for a quarter of an hour. I love these sweet, fiery pangs but I will not court them.' Nevertheless a few

years later in Samoa he sometimes made pre-prandial cocktails probably less explosive than this first specimen which — on internal evidence in two senses — sounds like the primitive cocktail technicaly known as an Old-Fashioned, not the insidiously pale Martini that California probably invented.

It is strange that with such lubrications at work and with his life committed to an American wife and family, the American figures in Stevenson's later novels are such botches in speech and to some degree in character. *The Ebb Tide* has an American principal figure. *The Wrecker* has two and much of its actions is laid in the States. It has long been notorious that from Mrs Trollope to Ian Fleming the British author writing lines for Americans has almost always failed miserably. I suppose charitably, though I am in no position to judge, that the converse may hold good of American writers putting words in British mouths. If Stevenson was aware of this hazard, he may have relied too much on Fanny and Lloyd Osbourne — who was his collaborator on both books — to correct anomalies in usage and syntax; and they have been too diffident to do so — though diffidence in such matters was not Fanny's normal way. In any case, I once counted fourteen errors of idiom in the first twelve pages of Chapter 1 of *The Wrecker*.

Yet we must be grateful for graces obscured by minor shortcomings. Both the *The Ebb Tide* and *The Wrecker* are creditable. For instance, between them they showed the way for much that would later make Joseph Conrad a considerable figure. *The Wrecker* contains an American principal, Jim Pinkerton. As type of the hyperkinetic, naively well meaning but opportunistic American entrepreneur, he leaves much to be desired, but it was in his American mouth that Stevenson fittingly put crucial evidence of what years and America between them did for the Gifted Boy of 17 Heriot Row. Pinkerton stands in respectful awe of what one now calls the Creative Impulse. But he is also bewildered by the singlemindedness with which most writers, painters and composers insist on manifesting it. To his American crony and partner, who is obsessed with the practice of art and finds all else a weariness, he protests: 'What I can't see is why you should want to do nothing else.' And the objection is let stand in contrast to the competing elder validity of

R.L.S.: last photograph

what Stevenson defines as 'the eternal life of man spent under sun and rain and in rude physical effort'.

A few years earlier he had said much the same in a piece written for an American magazine during his second stay in America, with the title *Letter to a Young Gentleman who Proposes to Embrace the Career of Art*. Henry James called this, 'a little mine of felicities'. So it is. Most writers who take themselves seriously would also consider it a rather explosive mine of heresies. Here in Stevenson's words are some of its unorthodox notions:

> . . . many thousand artists spend their lives, if the result be regarded, utterly in vain; a thousand artists, and never a work of art. But . . . the artist, even if he does not amuse the public, amuses himself; . . . what shall he enjoy more fully than a morning of successful work? Suppose it ill paid; the wonder is it should be paid at all. Other men pay, and pay dearly, for pleasures less desirable . . . making or swallowing artistic formulae, or perhaps falling in love with some particular proficiency . . . many artists forget the end of art: to please. It is doubtless tempting to exclaim against the ignorant bourgeois; yet . . . it is he who pays us, and that (surely on the face of it) for services that he shall desire to have performed . . . To give the public what they do not want, and yet expect to be supported . . . a strange pretention, and yet no uncommon, above all with painters . . . The first duty in this world is for a man to pay his way; when that is accomplished, he may plunge into what eccentricity he likes . . . Till then he must pay assiduous court to the bourgeois who carries the purse . . . if he be of a mind so independent that he cannot stoop to this necessity . . . he can desist from art, and follow some more manly way of life.

Then Stevenson gave his target the other barrel: '. . . a more manly way of life . . . a point on which I must be frank. To live by a pleasure is not a high calling; it involves patronage, however veiled; it numbers the artist, however ambitious, along with dancing-girls and billiard-markers. The French have a romantic evasion for one employment, and call its practitioners the Daughters of Joy. The artist is of the same family . . . It will be seen I have little sympathy with the common lamentations of the artist class . . .' Indeed and indeed.

He could have added that particularly the writer who, to Pinkerton's bewilderment, insists on doing nothing else is rather a newcomer. Until fairly recently, as the centuries go, the greatest writers in English wrote only incidentally to other careers. Those lacking funded income or indirect subsidy practiced lucrative professions as a sort of self-subsidy. Shakespeare was primarily an actor; Milton and Chaucer civil servants. Our Parnassus abounds in clergymen, lawyers, physicians, seamen, politicians. But that is only supplementary to Stevenson's severity, which seems to me as mature-minded a statement as a writer ever made about his craft. In my view Stevenson might never have come so far had he lacked the physical and emotional shock treatment that America afforded him. She kept a hard school; but she did shake him down — after shaking him up — into the still mercurial but admirably integrated man he became.